Contents

****

A STRAIGHTFORWARD GUIDE
TO
HOUSING RIGHTS

Roger Sproston BA, MSc

—

ı
.n t

To rer
or co'

Yo'

Straightforward Guides
www.straightforwardco.co.uk

British Library Cataloguing in Publication data. A Catalogue record of this book is available from the British Library.

ISBN

978-1-80236-053-0

Printed by 4 Edge www.4edge.co.uk

INTRODUCTION

This revised edition of A Guide to Housing Rights, **updated to 2022**, is a comprehensive overview of housing law and the rights of occupiers across three main tenures, Private sector tenants, public sector tenants and Owner occupiers. There is also a general section covering park homes, houseboats, and agricultural tenants. Private sector tenancies in Scotland are also covered.

However, if the reader requires more in-depth information concerning owner occupation in Scotland go to:

scotland.shelter.org.uk:

For Northern Ireland, advice about private tenants' rights and owner occupation can be obtained from www.housingadviceni.org.

Coronavirus temporary law changes

At the time of writing, we have passed the peak of the coronavirus epidemic, or at least the effects that the pandemic had on housing. Landlords are free to repossess properties and mortgage providers to foreclose. To date however, the 'Tsunami' of homelessness hasn't been as drastic as was envisaged.

Landlords have been warned to take note of the Minimum Energy Efficiency Standard regulation which came into force on 1 April 2020. The changes mean properties where tenancies pre-date April 2018 must have an Energy Performance Rating above E. When initially introduced in April 2018, all properties marketed for let were legally required to have an EPC (energy performance certificate) rating of E or above before the commencement of any new tenancies. However, the legislation will shortly be extended to also cover properties where current tenancies pre-date April 2018. Landlord regulatory requirements have not been relaxed during the coronavirus outbreak and financial penalties for non-compliance remain enforceable, with a potential fine of up to £5,000 per infraction.

The government had stated "Landlords should make every effort to ensure they are meeting at least the new minimum standards despite the logistical challenges imposed by the outbreak. It is vital to maintain open channels of communication with tenants to ensure that they are not vulnerable or self-isolating before proceeding with any essential work."

All evictions were suspended until March 31st, 2021, this affected mortgage holders as well as private and social renters across England and Wales.

The stay on possession proceedings expired on 20 September 2020 and landlords are now able to progress their possession claim through the courts. Courts will carefully prioritise the most egregious cases, such as those involving anti-social behaviour and other crimes. Longer notice periods and new court rules apply in all local tiers.

To protect against Coronavirus (COVID-19) transmission, the government changed the law to ensure bailiffs did not to enforce evictions in all local tiers in England until 11 January 2021. For a full breakdown of housing and coronavirus, and the situation in 2022, go to https://england.shelter.org.uk/housing_advice/coronavirus.

The information is up to date as at March 2022 and is comprehensive.

**

Housing is very complex and affects all people at some point in their lives. Housing law is ever changing and knowledge of it is usually outside the scope of the layperson. There is the problem now of housing, whether owner occupied or rented, being unaffordable, particularly in London and the Southeast. The whole free-for-all in the Housing Market, which really began in earnest with the reforms to the private sector and 'Buy to Let' in 1989, is now coming to an end. The Government is tightening up the private sector with increasing legislation and regulations designed to curb the activities of lettings agents.

The Tenant Fees Act 2019, which became law on 1st June 2019, stops estate agents charging exorbitant fees to tenants and affects tenants' deposits, Rules affecting Houses in Multiple Occupation, aimed at tightening up this area of housing came into effect from October 1st, 2018. Also, rules around private lettings and energy performance came into effect, and the introduction of new redress schemes for both tenants and owner occupiers. Local authorities too have been given increased powers to regulate private sector lettings in their areas.

From October 1st, 2018, the changes introduced by the Deregulation Act 2015 have been extended. These changes first came into effect on 1 October 2015 but only for tenancies which started or were renewed for new fixed terms after that date ('new tenancies'). Therefore, there has been a transition period for tenancies which pre-dated 1 October 2015 ('old tenancies'). This transition period ended on 1 October 2018 and from that date the Deregulation Act changes apply to all ASTs. This will be covered further on in the book.

Correspondingly, there is the increasing problem of homelessness and what to do at this traumatic time. How do local authorities work and what are their obligations towards the individual? What is the role of housing associations and housing co-operatives and how can one gain access to this type of property, particularly with the government historically intent on reducing the availability of social housing? To grapple with the problem of homelessness the government has introduced the Homelessness Reduction Act 2017, which became fully operative in April 2018. The Homelessness Reduction Act 2017 is one of the biggest changes to the rights of homeless people in England for 15 years. It effectively bolts two new duties to the original statutory rehousing duty:

- Duty to prevent homelessness

- Duty to relieve homelessness

In response to the introduction of this Act, Shelter states:

'But its (the 2017 Act) laudable aims to reduce homelessness will be undermined without improvements to wider housing and welfare policy, to address both the causes of homelessness and to ensure that homeless households have access to settled, affordable and suitable housing in each local authority area.

Without these improvements, there could be unintended consequences, such as 'gate-keeping' of services, unlawful decisions, increased out-of-area moves and repeat homelessness, with damaging consequences for children and other vulnerable applicants, and little improvement in meaningful outcomes for single adults'.

Leaseholders have been in the news, for several reasons, with the exposure of extortionate ground rents and the government has banned the sale of new build leasehold property. This is because property developers have been completing schemes and then selling on the freehold to companies who are able to profit from the outsize ground rents which in many cases render a property impossible to sell in the future. In addition, since the Grenfell House fire in 2017, and the revelation that cladding around the building had contributed to the rapid spread of the fire, there have been high profile cases where freeholders have tried to pass on the costs of stripping buildings to leaseholders, in some cases tens of thousands of pounds. The Government has, introduced the Fire Safety Act 2021 (effective from April 2021) and the Building Safety Bill that is making its way through Parliament in 2022. In addition, the government has now announced that many developers have signed up to an agreement that all costs of stripping buildings of cladding, plus any associated costs such as 'nightwatch' will be borne by developers and not leaseholders. This may, however, exclude buy-to-let landlords in a block.

One other element in the Building Safety Bill is that Leaseholders facing building safety remediation costs will be able to seek legal action for homes built up to 15 years ago.

Further, in January 2021, the government announced that leaseholders in England are to be given the right to extend their leases by up to 990 years at zero ground rent, in a move the government claims could save households tens of thousands of pounds.

The Ministry of Housing, Communities and Local Government said it is also working on establishing a Commonhold Council involving government, leasehold groups, and industry representatives to prepare the market for widespread take-up of commonhold.

The Government has also announced that the UK is to get a new housing complaints resolution service so that both homeowners and tenants know where to go when things go wrong. This is still waiting to be put into effect in 2022.

For the first time ever, private landlords will be legally required to join a housing redress scheme and the then Secretary of State for Housing James Brokenshire stated that it will boost protection for millions of tenants across the country.

According to Brokenshire (Housing minister at the time) it will potentially help millions by providing a straightforward way of getting help when faced with unresolved disputes about problems with their home, such as repairs and maintenance.

Under the new service dissatisfied homeowners and tenants will have simple and quick access to help when things go wrong with the service covering everything from broken boilers to cracks in walls.

And to protect the interests of homeowners who buy new build homes, the Government has also reiterated its commitment to establishing a New Homes Ombudsman which will champion home buyers, protect their interests, and hold developers to account.

Legislation will be brought forward at the earliest possible opportunity to require all new developers to belong to the Ombudsman.

Developers will also have to belong to the new body if they wish to participate in the Government's landmark Help to Buy scheme.

The Housing Complaints Resolution Service will be developed with a new Redress Reform Working Group made up of representatives from across the sector, working with industry and consumers.

One other move to protect leaseholders is that reforms have been proposed by the law commission which advocate that homeowner with long leases on flats, who already have the Right-To Manage (RTM) their flats is suggesting changes to make the system easier and more accessible and more certain. These include enabling leasehold houses, as well as flats, to qualify for RTM, permitting multi-block RTM on estates and removing restrictions on buildings which have more than 25 per cent commercial space.

Finally, what happens if a person is subject to domestic violence and flees home? What are the obligations of local authorities and housing associations currently? What happens if a relationship breaks down, what are the rights and obligations of the respective parties at a time like this? Also, what are the rights of people in non-traditional forms of housing such as park homes and residential houseboats? At the end of the book there is a section on how to obtain housing advice.

A Guide to Housing Rights covers all the main areas in relation to housing and will to be of assistance to individuals who are interested in housing and corresponding rights, as well as those who study housing law.

This book does not cover care-homes as a separate body of rights exists for this area. However, if more advice is needed about care homes go to:

https://england.shelter.org.uk/.../care_homes_for_older_people

****

Chapter 1

HOUSING IN CONTEXT

Renting and owner occupation

Residential property in the United Kingdom is divided into three broad sectors, owner occupation, private renting, and the public sector. The latter is becoming very scarce indeed, and the government and the public sector are working together, at long last, to address the shortage.

Currently, buying a home in many areas is still only an option for those who can afford the prices, find a deposit, and get a mortgage. We are in a market where most first-time buyers are still excluded from buying a home, particularly in the southern areas of the UK. The pattern changes as you move from the south-east to the Midlands and the North, with getting on to the housing ladder and finding more affordable rent still a possibility.

There are distinct advantages to buying a property if you can. They are as follows:

- When buying you will have a wider choice of property and areas, obviously depending on the price range you can afford.
- You will have more control over your home than when renting.
- You can only normally lose your home if you do not keep up your mortgage repayments.
- In the longer term, it can be cheaper than renting and over the years you will build up equity in the property until you eventually own it.

There are disadvantages to owning, as follows:

- The costs in the early years are usually higher than renting a property, particularly from a local authority or housing association, although usually lower than the private sector.
- There is an initial high cost to buying a house, whereas this is not the case with rented property.
- As an owner-occupier you will be responsible for all repairs and maintenance which can be expensive.
- There is very limited help with your housing costs if your income drops.

Renting property

Obviously, the ideal landlord from whom to rent is a local authority or a housing association. The advantages of this are:

- Costs are usually lower than the private sector and rents are regulated. However, rents are steadily climbing in the public sector. If your income drops you are usually eligible for housing benefit although there have been significant changes to benefit entitlement in the last few years. Most of the repairs and maintenance will be carried out by the landlord, from rental income.
- You will only lose your home if you breach the terms of the tenancy agreement.
- The public sector is non-profit making and will usually be good landlords.There are disadvantages to renting from a local authority or housing association.
- In many areas now there is a very long waiting list for properties. When and if you eventually are housed it may not be in an area of choice.

- The rent will gradually increase, reaching levels higher than those who own, and you will not build up any equity in your property.

Private landlords

With the advent of buy-to-let, private landlords have increased greatly over the last 30 years and have become the dominant sector following the 'credit crunch' of 2007. There are some advantages to renting from a private landlord. They are:

- There will be a wider choice of areas and properties than in the public sector if you have the means to rent them.
- There is rarely a waiting list.
- You can get help with your rent if your income drops. Most of the repairs and maintenance will be met by the landlord out of rent.

There are, as always, disadvantages to renting in the private sector:

- Rents can be very high. This is the case particularly in London and the southeast. They are now out of control.
- Rent will go up over time, usually more than the public sector.
- Tenants in the private sector have relatively limited protection. In the public sector, tenancies are usually for life, subject to breach of contract. Private sector tenants are in the weakest position, with six-month tenancies being the norm. There are moves to address this problem, with a call for longer tenancies. Scotland has been active in this area and has introduced new laws (see chapter on Scottish private tenancies.
- Private sector landlords are often poor landlords with scant knowledge of the law.

Different types of houses and tenancy will suit different people at different times of their lives, depending on their circumstances. There are many things to consider when deciding, these being outlined below.

Renting from a local authority

For a full breakdown of public sector tenants rights, and the full range of public sector tenancies, go to: https//england.shelter.org.publc sector rights.

Council homes are, along with housing association property and, in some cases, housing co-operatives, the most affordable type of housing. However, they are also the most difficult to obtain, particularly as there have been moves in the past to make it more difficult for the public sector to build affordable housing.

The allocation of council housing will depend on your need and those in the most need will usually be given priority over others. This has been a bone of contention for many years, however, as need is measured in a scientific way, with points allocated according to different circumstances. Most local authorities run a bidding system which has made it more difficult for people to both obtain or swap housing.

You can find out from the council housing department about how to go about making an application for housing. If you are being actively considered for an offer of housing, then the council will usually send someone to visit you. In most cases, it is necessary to reregister on the housing register each year, to keep an active list of those in need.

The housing register

Councils will keep a list or register of people who apply for housing. This has been a requirement for some years now. This register is also sometimes known as a 'waiting list' although this is misleading since length of time on the list is certainly not the only factor considered when it comes to being rehoused. In the main, councils now operate a list where people bid for housing in an area.

A council can decide that a person is not eligible for housing if they have been guilty of behaviour that would entitle them to evict that person as a council tenant.

People arriving from abroad

Some people from abroad are not allowed to register on the housing list. This includes people who are subject to immigration control, people who are allowed to stay subject to not benefiting from public funds and sponsored immigrants who have been in the United Kingdom for less than five years. Also, people who fail the habitual residence test for welfare benefits or who are in breach of EU Rights of Residence Directive. If a local authority refuses to put your name on the housing register, you have the right to ask them to review their decision within 21 days. There are special arrangements for asylum seekers who will be directed towards accommodation in limited areas of the country.

Homelessness

Local authorities have a legal duty to provide help to certain people who are homeless or threatened with homelessness. Generally, a person will qualify for help if they are 'eligible for assistance', legally homeless or threatened with homelessness and not intentionally homeless. In England, Wales, and Northern Ireland, they must also be in priority need. This test was abolished in Scotland on 31 December 2012. The local authority may also investigate whether a person has a local connection with the area.

Local social services authorities also have responsibility for some homeless people. They have a duty to provide accommodation for children and young people over 16 who are leaving care, or who are in need for other reasons.

Eligible for Assistance
Certain people who arrive in this country, or who are returning from a period living abroad do not qualify for housing under homelessness laws. For example, many asylum-seekers (but not all) are excluded, as is someone who has spent significant time living away from the UK even if they are a UK citizen.

The Homelessness Reduction Act 2017
As mentioned in the introduction, The Homelessness Reduction Act 2017 came into force in England on 3rd of April 2018, and brings in new duties for local authorities that aim to prevent homelessness. The Act amends the Housing Act 1996, which sets out what level of assistance must be provided to a person who is homeless. The Homelessness code of guidance has been updated to provide statutory guidance to local authorities.

The new legislation provides local authorities with an opportunity to further contribute to alleviating migrant destitution, as although people with no recourse to public funds will not be eligible for homelessness assistance under the Housing Act 1996, local authorities must ensure that information and advice about homelessness prevention and alternative support options is made available to everyone in the area. This will include how to access social services' support, which is provided to prevent destitution when families, vulnerable adults and young people leaving care are excluded from mainstream welfare support by their immigration status.

17

Relevant changes

- Local authorities must provide free advice and information about the help that is available for people who are homeless or threatened with homelessness, which everybody in the area can access, including people who are not eligible for further homelessness services because of their immigration status.
- People who make a homelessness application and are found to be ineligible should be referred to any appropriate support services that they may be entitled to.
- The period in which someone must be treated as being threatened with homelessness under the Housing Act 1996 will be extended from 28 to 56 days.
- A new prevention duty requires the local authority to take reasonable steps to prevent an eligible person who is threatened with homelessness within 56 days from becoming homelessness, either by arranging for them to remain in their current home or by securing accommodation elsewhere, for example, a private tenancy of at least six months.
- A new relief duty requires the local authority to take reasonable steps to help an eligible person to secure accommodation within 56 days if homelessness has not been prevented, or if a person requests assistance when they are already homeless. Temporary accommodation may be provided during the relief period to those who are in priority need, for example, families with children under 18, pregnant women and vulnerable adults.
- The local authority must establish a personalised housing plan that sets out the reasonable steps the person and council will take to help prevent or relieve homelessness following an assessment of the person or family's needs. If accommodation is not secured

during the relief period, then the local authority will decide whether the person or family is owed a full homelessness duty.

- To comply with section 11 of the Children Act 2004, local authority housing departments must safeguard and promote the welfare of children and cooperate with other agencies, including social services. Local authorities must ensure that the child's needs are paramount, and the welfare, needs and wishes of each child should be put first, so that every child receives the support they need.
- Local authorities must review and publish a homelessness strategy, which should include input from social services to ensure that the needs of families and vulnerable adults who are threatened with homelessness are adequately considered within the strategy.

Implementing the changes - best practice

To comply with the Homelessness Reduction Act 2017 and cooperation duties set out in the Care Act 2014 and Children Act 2004, social services will need to:

- work effectively with the local authority's housing department (or district councils in two-tier authorities), to contribute to the homelessness strategy and provide relevant information to residents, prevent homelessness where this is a realistic outcome, and comply with the new referral duty.

Homelessness prevention

The new prevention and relief duties provide an opportunity for people to avoid having to move multiple times or spend a long period in temporary accommodation when their current home or alternative housing can be secured for them.

19

Other rights to re-housing

People who lose their homes because of action by the local authority will, usually, have a right to re-housing. Councils may make a compulsory purchase order on a house and then demolish it, councils may decide that a property needs improving and occupiers have to move out permanently. If this is the case, then there is a right to re-housing. Anyone legally living in the property at the time of these actions is entitled to re-housing, the right applying to owners or tenants. It does not apply to those moving in after the action has commenced or to squatters.

People who have to vacate their homes in these circumstances can also claim home loss payment to a maximum of £15,000, (check current figures with your local authority as they are subject to change) disturbance payment to help with the costs of moving and a well-maintained payment which involves a payment to the owners or tenants if the property is to be compulsory purchased and has been well maintained up to the time of compulsory purchase.

Other council housing schemes in operation

In addition to those schemes outlined above, councils have several other schemes in operation. The most common are Hard-to-let or low-demand schemes. This is where the council has unpopular homes in areas that are blighted for example, or in tower blocks. Property like this is typically offered to low priority groups such as young single people. However, hard to let schemes in London are impossible to find in 2020.

Schemes for special groups-Some council's have quotas for special groups, such as for those with special needs, mental illness etc.

Exchanging properties

Tenants of public sector housing, at least secure and assured tenants, have the right to exchange their homes with another person or family, subject to permission from the landlord, which cannot be unreasonably withheld. There are several reasons why the council or association can refuse to let an exchange go ahead:

- There is a court order to evict one of the applicants
- There is impending possession proceedings
- The accommodation you want to transfer is larger than your needs (substantially larger)
- The accommodation is too small
- The landlord is a charity, and the proposed new tenant does not suit the aims and objectives of the landlord
- Accommodation is specially adapted for a person with physical disabilities and the proposed new tenant is not disabled.
- The accommodation is managed by a tenant management co-operative and the proposed tenant does not want to become part of the co-operative.

Housing associations

Housing associations and housing trusts are slightly different to councils in their make up. Although publicly funded and accountable to a board of management and to Homes England (formerly the Homes and Communities Agency (HCA) until January 2018), which regulates the activities of associations, they are more independent than councils.

Housing associations will offer a variety of tenancy types, some not offered by councils. However, they will work closely with the local authority when it comes to receiving nominations and referrals for housing. Often, they are only permitted to develop in a local authority

21

area if they agree an ongoing quota of nominations from councils. Many associations will only house those on the housing register. However, if you have a problem getting onto the housing register then you should seek advice form the council.

Housing associations which are registered with the HCA are obliged by law to give details of how they allocate tenancies. Some associations will take direct applications others will work through agencies. It depends on the associations.

Housing association tenancies are usually assured and assured shorthold, with some secure, usually created out of an exchange. However, as we will see a little later, housing associations have not been able to grant secure tenancies since January 1st, 1989, and therefore, the secure tenancy, which is now a local authority tenancy only, is dwindling in associations.

Housing co-operatives

Housing co-operatives consist of groups of people who each have a share in the overall co-op, usually a £1 share and each have a responsibility for managing the co-op, usually delegated to a committee. Individuals are expected to show an active interest and participate in the day-to-day running. Co-ops will allocate their own property but will also sometimes have agreements with local authorities. Three are relatively few co-ops in existence and they are difficult to get into.

Renting from a private landlord

As we have seen above, if you cannot afford to buy a property, as a lot of people cannot be due to rising house prices, and you do not qualify for a council or housing association tenancy then you will need to do as a growing number of people do, and that is rent from a private

22

landlord. This is usually the most expensive way of renting but there is usually availability of property.

Most private lets are found through local estate agents with a letting arm. They will advertise property and vet prospective tenants, taking up references and provide a management service to the landlord that can cost anything between 10-15% of rental income plus VAT. Many agencies will charge the tenant a fee for drawing up a tenancy but are not allowed to charge a deposit before a property is found. However, the government announced in 2017 that lettings agents will be barred from charging tenants' fees. This came into effect on June 1st, 2019. Deposits will also be affected as outlined in chapter 3. On finding a property you will need to pay a deposit which is returnable. The deposit is now protected by the Tenancy Deposit Protection Scheme, introduced in 2007. Renting a property is outlined in more depth further on in the book.

Rogue landlords

The Housing and Planning Act 2016 introduced a range of measures to tackle rogue landlords who breach health and safety regulations, engage in illegal eviction and so on:

- civil penalties of up to £30,000 as an alternative to prosecution – came into force April 2017

- extension of Rent Repayment Orders to cover illegal eviction and/ or failure to comply with a statutory notice – came into force in April 2017. Rent Repayment Orders will also cover breach of a banning order from 6 April 2018.

Government has worked with Karen Buck MP to draft and publish the Private Member's Bill on Homes (Fitness for Human Habitation and

Liability of Housing Standards). The following guidance for local housing authorities has been published:

- the database of rogue landlords and property agents (which came into force on 6th April 2018)
- banning orders
- civil penalties
- rent repayment orders

Private lettings and Selective licensing

How Selective Licensing operates
Where selective licensing applies, unlike the other forms of licensing which relate to HMOs (Housing in Multiple Occupation, see chapter on Repairing obligations for more details on HMO's) then normally all houses within the private rented sector for that area must be licensed, except where they require to be licensed as HMOs. Non licensable HMOs must be licensed under Selective Licensing. "House" means a building or part of a building consisting of one or more dwellings. For those purposes "dwelling" means a building or part of a building occupied or intended to be occupied as a separate dwelling

Designation for Selective Licensing
Selective licensing is dependent on a designation by the local authority. A local authority may designate the whole of their district or part of their district, subject to selective licensing. An area may be designated for selective licensing either (i) if the area is (or is likely to be) an area of low housing demand **or** (ii) the area is experiencing a significant and persistent problem caused by anti social behaviour and some or all the private sector landlords are failing to take action to combat the
24

problem that it will be appropriate for them to take. A designation can last for five years. It can be renewed.

There are prescribed publicity requirements for designations and the revocation of designations.

Properties to which Selective Licensing applies

Selective licenses are required for houses within the designated area where the whole of the house is occupied either under a single tenancy or licence or under two or more tenancies or licences in respect of different dwellings contained in it.

Are there any exemptions?

A tenancy or licence is exempt from the selective licensing if it is granted by a registered social landlord.

The following tenancies/licences are also exempt where:

- a prohibition order is in force
- business tenancies
- licensed premises (for liquor licensing purposes)
- agricultural tenancies
- the property is managed/controlled by a local housing authority or public body
- the building is regulated under other legislation (e.g. care homes)
- the building is occupied by students controlled/managed by a University/College (who subscribe to an Approved Code of Practice)
- the occupier is a Member of The Family of the landlord/licensor who himself holds under a lease of the property for a minimum of 21 years
- holiday lets

- the occupier shares any amenity (i.e., a toilet bathroom kitchen or living room) with the landlord/licensor or a Member of The Family of the landlord/licensor

Temporary exemptions
if the landlord is taking steps to change the situation so that the property will no longer need to be licensed.

Differences between Selective Licensing and HMO Licensing
Generally, the same rules apply when granting a Selective Licence as with an HMO licence. The main differences are: -

- It is mandatory to take up references for a prospective tenant before letting a property subject to Selective Licensing.
- Unlike HMOs the licence authority does not have to consider suitability for letting or amenity standards when granting a selective licence. However, the licence holder must still be a fit and proper person.

****

Chapter 2

LANDLORD AND TENANT-THE LAW GENERALLY

Having looked at the housing market, and the main players generally, it is now necessary to outline the fundamentals of the law as it applies to landlord and tenant.

Explaining the law

It is very important for both landlords and tenants to understand the rights and obligations of respective parties to a tenancy and exactly what can and what cannot be done once the tenancy agreement has been signed and the property is occupied.

Some landlords think they can do exactly as they please because the property belongs to them. Some tenants do not know any differently and therefore the landlord can, and often does, get away with breaking the law. However, this is not the case, there is a very strong legal framework governing the relationship between landlord and tenant and it is important that both parties have a grasp on the key principles of the law.

In order to fully understand the law, we should begin by looking at the main types of relationship between people and their homes.

The freehold and the lease

In law, there are two main types of ownership and occupation of property. These are:

- freehold and.
- leasehold. These arrangements are very old indeed.

Freehold

If a person owns their property outright (usually with a mortgage) then they are a freeholder. The only claims to ownership over and above their own might be those of the building society or the bank, which lent them the money to buy the place. They will re-possess the property if the mortgage payments are not kept up with. In addition, the Crown can exercise rights in times of war, for example.

In certain situations, though, the local authority (council) for an area can affect a person's right to do what they please with their home even if they are a freeholder. This will occur when planning powers are exercised, for example, to prevent the carrying out of alterations without consent.

The local authority for your area has many powers and we will be referring to these regularly.

Leasehold

If a person lives in a property owned by someone else and has a written agreement allowing them to occupy the flat or house for a period i.e., giving them permission to live in that property, then they will, in the main, have a lease and either be a leaseholder or a tenant of a landlord.

The main principle of a lease is that a person has been given permission by someone else to live in his or her property for a period. The person giving permission could be either the freeholder or another leaseholder.

The tenancy agreement is one type of lease. If you have signed a tenancy agreement then you will have been given permission by a person to live in their property for a period.

The position of the tenant

The tenant will usually have an agreement for a shorter period than the typical leaseholder. Whereas the leaseholder will, for example, have an agreement for ninety-nine years, the tenant will have an agreement, which either runs from week to week or month to month (periodic tenancy) or is for a fixed term, for example, six-months or one-year. These arrangements are the most common types of agreement between the private landlord and tenant. The agreement itself will state whether it is a fixed-term or periodic tenancy. If an agreement has not been issued it will be assumed to be a fixed term tenancy. Both periodic and fixed-term tenants will usually pay a sum of rent regularly to a landlord in return for permission to live in the property (more about rent and service charges later)

The tenancy agreement

The tenancy agreement is the usual arrangement under which one person will live in a property owned by another. Before a tenant moves into a property, he/she will have to sign a tenancy agreement drawn up by a landlord or landlord's agent. *A tenancy agreement is a contract between landlord and tenant.* It is important to realize that when you sign a tenancy agreement, you have signed a contract with another person, which governs the way in which you will live in their property.

The contract

Typically, any tenancy agreement will show the name and address of the landlord and will state the names of the tenant(s). The type of tenancy agreement that is signed should be clearly indicated. This could be, for example, a Rent Act protected tenancy, an assured tenancy or an assured shorthold tenancy. In the main, in the private sector, the agreement will be an assured shorthold.

Date of commencement of tenancy and rent payable

The date the tenancy began and the duration (fixed term or periodic) plus the amount of rent payable should be clearly shown, along with who is responsible for any other charges, such as water rates, council tax etc, and a description of the property you are living in.

The landlord must also serve a notice stating the address to where any legal notices can be sent. In addition to the rent that must be paid there should be a clear indication of when a rent increase can be expected. This information is sometimes shown in other conditions of tenancy, which should be given to the tenant when they move into their home. The conditions of tenancy will set out landlords and tenants rights and obligations.

Services provided under the tenancy and service of notice

If services are provided, i.e., if a service charge is payable, this should be indicated in the agreement. The tenancy agreement, as stated, should clearly indicate the address to which notices on the landlord can be served by the tenant, for example, because of repair problems or notice of leaving the property. The landlord has a legal requirement to indicate this.

Tenants' obligations

The tenancy agreement will either be a basic document with the above information or will be more comprehensive. Either way, there will be a section beginning "the tenant agrees." Here the tenant will agree to move into the property, pay rent, use the property as an only home, not cause a nuisance to others, take responsibility for certain internal repairs, not sublet the property, i.e., create another tenancy, and various other things depending on the property.

Landlords' obligations

There should also be another section "the landlord agrees". Here, the landlord is contracting with the tenant to allow quiet enjoyment of the property. The landlord's repairing responsibilities are also usually outlined.

Ending a tenancy through a ground for possession

Finally, there should be a section entitled "ending the tenancy" which will outline the ways in which landlord and tenant can end the agreement. If it is an assured shorthold tenancy then a Form 6A notice will be served to end the tenancy naturally, the same for ending on a ground, such as rent arrears (Form 6A has replaced s21 and s8 notices for all tenancies from October 1st, 2018) more about this later). It is in this section that the landlord should refer to the "grounds for possession". Grounds for possession are circumstances where the landlord will apply to court for possession of his/her property. Some of these grounds relate to what is in the tenancy, i.e., the responsibility to pay rent and to not cause a nuisance. Other grounds do not relate to the contents of the tenancy directly, but more to the law governing that tenancy. The grounds for possession are very important, as they are used in any court case brought against the tenant. Unfortunately, they are not always indicated in the tenancy agreement. As they are so important, they are summarized later on in this chapter.

It must be said at this point that many residential tenancies are very light on landlord's responsibilities. Repairing responsibilities, and responsibilities relating to rental payment, are landlord's obligations under law. This book deals with these, and other areas. However, many landlords will seek to use only the most basic document to conceal legal obligations.

The public sector tenancy (local authority or housing association), for example, is usually very clear and very comprehensive about the rights and obligations of landlord and tenant. Unfortunately, the private landlord often does not employ the same energy when it comes to educating and informing the tenant.

Overcrowding /too many people living in the property

It is important to understand, when signing a tenancy agreement, that it is not permitted to allow the premises to become overcrowded, i.e., to allow more people than was originally intended, (which is outlined in the agreement) to live in the property. If a tenant does, then the landlord can take action to evict.

By the same token, landlords are faced with new regulations (since 2017 – see below) that they do not create overcrowding. Rogue landlords will be banned from cramming tenants into tiny box rooms in a government initiative to improve housing standards. Rooms must be no smaller than 70sq ft for a single person and 110sq ft for couples, under new rules announced by the Department for Communities. Rogue landlords who rent out substandard properties face being forced out of the sector as new banning orders are brought in and a national database of offenders went live on 6th April 2018.

The crackdown comes after an investigation by a newspaper last year found rogue landlords converting two- or three-bedroom terraced homes into bedsits that house eight or more strangers, each paying £400 to £500 a month for a room. Animal infestations are common and many of the homes have unsafe electrics and are damp. Fire precautions are mostly non-existent. Such overcrowding has caused tensions within communities with neigbours complaining of noise and anti-social behaviour and rubbish over-flowing from small front yards.

Councils will be able to use revenue from the licence fee to enforce the higher standards, with fines of up to £30,000 for the worst offenders.

Different types of tenancy agreement
The protected tenancy - the meaning of the term
As a basic guide, if a person is a private tenant and signed their current agreement with a landlord before 15th January 1989 then they will, in most cases, be a protected tenant with all the rights relating to protection of tenure, which are considerable. Protection is provided under the 1977 Rent Act. In practice, there are not many protected tenancies left and the tenant will usually be signing an assured shorthold tenancy.

The assured shorthold tenancy - what it means
If the tenant entered into an agreement with a landlord after 15th January 1989, then they will, in most cases, be an assured tenant. We will discuss assured tenancies in more depth in the next chapter In brief, there are various types of assured tenancy. The assured shorthold is usually a fixed term version of the assured tenancy and enables the landlord to recover their property after six months and to vary the rent after this time.

At this point it is important to understand that the main difference between the two types of tenancy, protected and assured, is that the tenant has less rights as a tenant under the assured tenancy. For example, they will not be entitled, as is a protected tenant, to a fair rent set by a Rent Officer.

Other types of agreement
In addition to the above tenancy agreements, there are other types of

33

agreement sometimes used in privately rented property. One of these is the company let, as we discussed in the last chapter, and another is the license agreement. The person signing such an agreement is called a licensee.

Licenses will only apply in special circumstances where the licensee cannot be given sole occupation of his home and therefore can only stay for a short period with minimum rights. There is one other type of agreement that is not widely used and that is the Common law tenancy.

Common Law Tenancies

These are tenancies that fall outside the scope of the Housing Acts (1988, 1996, 2004), which includes Regulated Tenancies, Assured Tenancies (AT) and Assured Shorthold Tenancies ASTs.

In the case of common law tenancies, the tenant's rights and obligations are mainly dependent on the terms agreed between the parties (written into the agreement), and therefore like a commercial lease; they are contractual or "non-statutory contractual tenancies" as opposed to those being regulated by statute.

Commercial (business tenancies) are similar, but businesses have the added protection of the Landlord and Tenant Act 1954, which affords some security of tenure (succession rights) for a business on renewal – when the fixed term comes to an end.

Any residential tenancy where the rent equates to an **annual rate more than £100,000 pa** (previously £25,000 set in 1990 and increased in October 2010) is excluded from the Housing Act Tenancy (AT or AST) rules and therefore must be a common law tenancy.

Alternatively, where a limited company rents a residential property (usually for their employees) the tenancy will fall outside the scope of the Housing Acts – again it's a common law tenancy.

Often, companies rent residential accommodation and let the property to their employees, usually under a licence agreement (as opposed to a tenancy). Often the employee pays rent and other costs to the landlord, but ultimately the company is liable.

Joint Tenancies and The Common Law Tenancy
A rental rate of £100,000 pa may seem quite a lot, but this also applies to join tenancies where the combined rent of all the sharers (such as students) is included in this total - £8333.33 per month is the limit.

Implications for Landlords – Common Law Tenancies
The implications of common law tenancies are:
(1) a different tenancy agreement from the usual AST will be required, and
(2) any deposit taken is not subject to the requirements of the Deposit Protection Scheme under the Housing Act 2004.
(3) the rules governing re-possession under the Housing Acts do not apply.

Security of Tenure – Common Law Tenancies
Common Law Tenancies do not afford tenants the same protection regarding security of tenure and statutory continuation as do Assured Tenancies (including Shorthold Assured Tenancies).

Therefore, the AST section 21 and section 8 notices and possession procedures do not apply, and the letting operates on the literal wording of the Tenancy Agreement. Similarly, the Deposit Protection (DPS Scheme) rules do not apply. However, the Protection from Eviction Act 1977 still applies, meaning that in the case of a common law residential tenant refusing to leave, a court order will be required.

Bringing a Common Law Tenancy to an End
With a Common Law tenancy, the landlord is entitled to possession at the end of the fixed term. In theory the landlord is not required to serve a notice to quit to bring the tenancy to an end as the tenancy ends at the agreed date, but in practice the landlord should serve a notice if he wishes the tenant to vacate.

Also, if there are problems during the tenancy, the landlord can bring the common law tenancy to an end where there has been a breach of any of the specified terms in the tenancy agreement. He is not restricted to the prescribed terms (grounds) laid down in Housing Acts.

Statutory Protection for Common Law Tenants
A residential common law tenant still has some statutory protection in that they cannot be evicted against their will unless the landlord obtains a court order (Protection from Eviction Act 1977).

Common Law Tenants will also get protection under the Unfair Terms in Consumer Contracts Regulations 1999, where they have entered a standard form (pre-printed) tenancy agreement.

They will also benefit from some other statutory provisions including the landlord's repairing obligations under the Landlord and Tenant Act 1985.

Squatting
Under section 144 of the Legal Aid, Sentencing and Punishment of Offenders Act, which came into force on the first day of September 2012, squatting in residential buildings (like a house or flat) is illegal. It can lead to 6 months in prison, a £5,000 fine, or both. Squatting is when someone knowingly enters a residential building as a trespasser and lives there or intends to live there.

A tenant who enters a property with the permission of the landlord, but who falls behind with rent payments, is **not** a squatter. Although squatting a non-residential building or land isn't in itself a crime, trespassers on non-residential property may be committing other crimes.

It's normally a crime for a person to enter private property without permission and refuse to leave when the owner asks. In certain circumstances, it may also be a crime if someone doesn't leave land when they've been directed to do so by the police or council, or if they don't comply with a repossession order.

Squatting in non-residential properties
A non-residential property is any building or land that isn't designed to be lived in.

Simply being on another person's non-residential property without their permission is not usually a crime. But if squatters commit other crimes when entering or staying in a property, the police can act against them. These crimes could include:

- causing damage when entering the property
- causing damage while in the property
- not leaving when they're told to by a court
- stealing from the property
- using utilities like electricity or gas without permission
- fly-tipping
- not complying with a noise abatement notice

Getting a non-residential property back
If a person owns the property that has been squatted, he or she can use an interim possession order (IPO) to get their property back quickly.

Court action

If the right procedure is followed, they can usually get one issued by the courts within a few days. To get final possession of the property, they must also make an application for possession when they apply for the IPO.

Use form N130 to apply for an interim possession order and for possession.

Exceptions

You can't use an IPO if:

- you're also making a claim for damages caused by the squatters - instead you can make an ordinary claim for possession
- more than 28 days have passed since you found out about the squatters
- you're trying to evict former tenants, sub-tenants, or licensees. Once squatters are served with an IPO, they must leave the property within 24 hours. If they don't, they're committing a crime and could serve up to 6 months in prison.

It's also a crime for them to return to the property within 12 months.

Squatters taking ownership of a property

It's difficult and very rare for squatters to take ownership of a property. To do this, they would have to stay in a property without the owner's permission for at least 10 years.

****

Chapter 3

PRIVATE TENANTS-FINDING PROPERTY

Letting Agents

One of the first places a prospective private tenant will look to rent a property is a lettings agent. It is important to know what the rules are governing agents as, particularly since the rise in demand for private properties, agents started to use unscrupulous methods to extract more money from tenants and landlords, but particularly tenants,

An amendment to the Enterprise and Regulatory Reform Act 2013 enabled the Government to require agents to sign up to a redress scheme. *The Redress Scheme for Lettings Agency Work and Property Management Work (Requirement to Belong to a Scheme etc) (England) Order 2014* made membership of a scheme a legal requirement with effect from 1 October 2014. There have been moves since 2020 to introduce a further tenant's redress scheme.

The Tenant Fees Act 2019 came into effect in June 2019 along with new rules covering deposits. A deposit will be limited to five weeks, where annual rent is below £50,000 with new, stricter rules on holding deposits. The new rules apply to all tenancies signed after 01 June 2019.

The Clients Protection Money Scheme 2019

These schemes make sure landlords and tenants are compensated if agents cannot repay their money, for example if they go into administration. This is different to tenancy deposit protection.

Agents may be fined up to £30,000 if they do not join a client money protection scheme.

The rules are different in:
- Scotland
- Wales - agents need to join a money protection scheme before they apply for an agent licence through Rent Smart Wales
- Northern Ireland - agents do not have to join a client money protection scheme

Approved schemes
Agents can join any of the following approved schemes:
- Client Money Protect
- Money Shield
- Propertymark
- RICS
- Safeagent (previously NALS)
- UKALA Client Money Protection

Agents must:
- hold their clients' money in an account with a bank or building society authorised by the Financial Conduct Authority
- get a certificate confirming membership of the scheme they join, and provide it to anyone who asks, free of charge

Agents need to display the certificate:

- in any office where they deal with the public
- on their website

Agents may be fined up to £5,000 if they do not display a certificate of membership or provide it when asked.

Online lettings agents

The rise of online lettings agents has been rapid and they now account for 3.5% of the market. The attractions are obvious, the costs. One of the biggest online property agents, EasyProperty.com offers 'pick and mix' services ranging from £10 a week for adverts on Right Move, Prime Location and Zoopla to 3% commission for full property management. For tenant finding with all the frills, such as hosted viewings and professional photos, in the total bill would be £445. This equates to less than half the commission charged by high-street agents. Another agent, Purplebricks.com is also very competitive. However, Purplebricks has overextended itself recently (2022) and has entered the area of lettings agency with disastrous results.

Activities of letting agents

Typically, a (good) letting agent will take responsibility for:

1. Transferring the utility bills and the council tax into the name of the tenant. Sign agreements and take up references.
2. Paying for repairs, although an agent will only normally do this if rent is being paid directly to them and they can make appropriate deductions.
3. Chasing rent arrears.Serving notices of intent to seek possession if the landlord instructs them to do so. An agent cannot commence court proceedings except through a solicitor.

41

4. Visiting the property at regular intervals and check that the tenants are not causing any damage.
5. Dealing with neighbour complaints.
6. Banking rental receipts if the landlord is abroad
7. Dealing with housing benefit departments if necessary. The extent to which agents do any or all the above really depends on the calibre of the agent. It also depends on the type of agreement you have with the agent.

Immigration Act 2014 and checking eligibility to rent
In October 2014, the Immigration Act 2014 came into force which puts the responsibility on landlords to vet their tenants, or prospective tenants to check to see if they have a right to be in the country (the obligation came into force in February 2016). Only when this is verified can a letting go ahead. More information about the Right to Rent checks can be obtained from:
https://www.gov.uk/landlord-immigration-check

Company lets
Where the tenant is a company rather than an individual, the tenancy agreement will be like an assured shorthold but will not be bound by the six-month rule (see chapter eight for details of assured shorthold tenancies). Company lets can be from any length of time, from a week to several years, or as long as you like.

The major difference between contracts and standard assured shorthold agreements is that the contract will be tailored to individual needs, and the agreement is bound by the provisions of contract law. Company tenancies are bound by the provisions of contract law and not by the Housing Acts.

Short lets

Short lets are only applicable in large cities where there is a substantial shifting population. Business executives on temporary relocation, actors and others involved in television production or film work, contract workers and visiting academics are examples of people who might require a short let. From a landlord's point of view, short lets are an excellent idea if they must vacate your own home for seven or eight months, say, and do not want to leave it empty. Short-let tenants provide useful extra income as well as keeping an eye on the place. Or if you are buying a new property and have not yet sold the old one, it can make good business sense to let it to a short-let tenant.

Short-let tenants are, usually, from a landlord's point of view, excellent blue-chip occupants. They are busy professionals, high earners, out all day and used to high standards. As the rent is paid by the company there is no worry for the landlord on this score either.

A major plus of short lets is that they command between 20-50 percent more rent than the optimum market rent for that type of property. The one downside of short lets is that no agency can guarantee permanent occupancy.

Student lets

Many mainstream letting agencies will not consider students and a lot of landlords similarly are not keen. There is the perception that students will not look after a home and tend to live a lifestyle guaranteed to increase the wear and tear on a property. However, several specialist companies have grown up which concentrate solely on students. Although students quite often want property for only eight or nine months, agencies that deal with students make them sign for a whole year. Rent is guaranteed by confirmation that the student is a genuine student with references from parents, who act as guarantors.

Holiday lets

The key rules and regulations that apply to holiday/short-term lets: For a property to count as a holiday let, it must be furnished and available for letting for at least 210 days a year. That means an owner can use it for up to 22 weeks.

To benefit from the favourable 'furnished holiday let' tax status, the property must be commercially let for at least 105 days in the year. Certain services must be provided for the let to be deemed a holiday let. Cleaning services and changes of bed linen are essential. The amount paid by the holidaymaker will usually include utilities but would exclude use of the telephone, fax machine etc.

Bedsits

Bedsitting rooms are usually difficult to let and can cause problems. There are numerous regulations to adhere to.

The Housing Act 2004, and subsequent rules, introduced tougher regulations for HMOs. If a landlord is letting out property in a block with more than three unrelated dwellings, then a licence will be needed from the local authority before lettings can take place. (See chapter on repairs for more details about HMO's)

Landlords taking in a lodger

One way of finding accommodation is to approach people, through websites listed below, who wish to take in a lodger. The following are the main points to consider:

- Under the current Rent a Room Scheme a person can earn rental income of up to £7,500 a year (£625 a month from 2022/23) from a furnished room in their house, without having to pay tax on it. This reduces to £3,750 if someone else receives income from letting accommodation in the same property, such as a joint owner. The limit is the same even if you let accommodation for less than 12 months.

- Prospective Landlords can find lodgers using listings websites such as uk.easyroommate.com, mondaytofriday.com and spareroom.co.uk or fivenights.com (as their names suggest, the last two sites specialise in lodgers who need only weekday accommodation).

- A lodger may be a friend or relation; in other cases, its important to vet anyone thoroughly before they move in. Experian, the credit reference agency, offers a tenants' screening service, under which a landlord can check a prospective tenant's identity, references, and ability to pay the rent. The service costs from £15-£25. The prospective tenant must give permission for his or her detail to be shared with you.

- A prospective landlord has certain responsibilities for example, they need to ensure that their gas appliances have been tested for safety. For more details go to gassaferegister.co.uk

- A prospective landlord may prefer to dispense with a legal agreement with your lodger but, if they prefer a more formal relationship, they can download the necessary documentation from lawpack.co.uk The agreement should set out every detail of how the arrangement will work, including rent, what parts of the house the lodger can use, whether guests can stay overnight, and on what basis the arrangement can be terminated.

- If the landlord shares their kitchen, bathroom or living room with a lodger, you can evict this person at any time – giving reasonable notice. This is normally 28 days. Under the law, the lodger is viewed as an "excluded occupier" rather than as a tenant. For more on this, see the government website: gov.uk/rent-room-in-your-home/the-rent-a-room-scheme

- A prospective landlord should notify their home and contents insurer and their mortgage lender before taking in a lodger. If they are a tenant themselves, subletting a room in this way could give rise to problems: they should check their own tenancy agreement.

- The Airbnb website enables people to let a room – or whole property – hotel-style, on an ad hoc basis. landlords can charge considerably higher rates per night than they would charge a lodger, and there is greater flexibility as they may choose to let a room for only a few weeks a year. Airbnb hosts with stylish properties in London can charge £150-plus a night for a large bedroom with en suite, but guests expect standards commensurate with prices.

- It is free to advertise rooms on airbnb.co.uk. The company sends a photographer to take pictures for your listing. Hosts use the Airbnb site's software to manage bookings, and they pay commission of 3per cent on each accepted reservation. Similar websites include Wimdu. However, Revenue & Customs could consider that regular hosts are running a business, so check before assuming that earnings qualify for the Rent a Room Scheme.

Deposits-Tenancy Deposit Protection Scheme

The Tenancy Deposit Protection Scheme was introduced to protect all deposits paid to landlords (except landlords of common law tenancies such as company lets) after 6th April 2007. After this date, landlords and/or agents must use a government authorised scheme to protect deposits. The need for such a scheme has arisen because of the historical problem with deposits. (As mentioned, deposits are now limited to five weeks, where annual rent is below £50,000 with new, stricter rules on holding deposits. The new rules apply to all tenancies signed after 1st June 2019). The scheme works as below.

Moving into a property

At the beginning of a new tenancy agreement, the tenant will pay a deposit to the landlord or agent as usual. Within 14 days the landlord is required to give the tenant details of how the deposit is going to be protected including:

- the contact details of the tenancy deposit scheme
- the contact details of landlord or agent
- how to apply for the release of the deposit
- what to do if there is a dispute about the deposit

There are three tenancy deposit schemes that a landlord can opt for:
Tenancy Deposit Solutions Ltd
www.mydeposits.co.uk
info@mydeposits.co.uk
0333 321 m9401
The Tenancy Deposit Scheme
www.tds.gb.com
0845 226 7837

The Deposit Protection Service
www.depositprotection.com
0870 707 1 707

The schemes above fall into two categories, insurance-based schemes, and custodial schemes.

Custodial Scheme
- The tenant pays the deposit to the landlord
- The landlord pays the deposit into the scheme
- Within 14 days of receiving the deposit, the landlord must give the tenant prescribed information
- A the end of the tenancy, if the landlord and tenant have agreed how much of the deposit is to be returned, they will tell the scheme which returns the deposit, divided in the way agreed by the parties.
- If there is a dispute, the scheme will hold the disputed amount until the dispute resolution service or courts decide what is fair
- The interest accrued by deposits in the scheme will be used to pay for the running of the scheme and any surplus will be used to offer interest to the tenant, or landlord if the tenant isn't entitled to it.

Insurance based schemes
- The tenant pays the deposit to the landlord
- The landlord retains the deposit and pays a premium to the insurer (this is the key difference between the two schemes)
- Within 14 days of receiving a deposit the landlord must give the tenant prescribed information.

- At the end of the tenancy if the landlord and tenant agree how the deposit is to be divided or otherwise then the landlord will return the amount agreed
- If there is a dispute, the landlord must hand over the disputed amount to the scheme.
- If for any reason the landlord fails to comply, the insurance arrangements will ensure the return of the deposit to the tenant if they are entitled to it.

If a landlord or agent hasn't protected a deposit with one of the above, then the tenant can apply to the local county court for an order for the landlord either to protect the deposit or repay it.

If you don't rent your home on an assured shorthold tenancy, your landlord can accept valuable items (for example a car or watch) as a deposit instead of money. The items won't be protected by a scheme.

The Deregulation Act 2015
Since 6 April 2007, it has been mandatory for a landlord to ensure that a tenant's deposit that has been paid in respect of an assured shorthold tenancy (AST) is protected within a Tenancy Deposit Scheme. The Deregulation Act now extends the requirement to protect a deposit to AST's created before 6 April 2007 in certain circumstances. Landlords are now required to protect their deposits within a scheme and serve the prescribed information relating to the deposit on the tenant. If a landlord fails to do this, then it is prevented from recovering possession of the property from the tenant and is potentially liable for financial penalties.

Rental guarantees

The landlord is always advised to obtain a guarantor if there is any potential uncertainty as to payment of rent. One example is where the tenant is on benefits. The guarantor will be expected to assume responsibility for the rent if the tenant ceases to pay at any time during the term of the tenancy.

****

Chapter 4

ASSURED TENANTS

Most people, when renting a property through the private sector will hold an assured shorthold tenancy, which is a derivation of an assured tenancy. In this chapter we will elaborate on the exact nature of these tenancies.

The assured tenant

As we have seen, except for local authority secure tenancies, and also various other types of agreements, such as company lets, all tenancies, are known as assured tenancies. An assured shorthold, which is the most common form of tenancy used by the private landlord nowadays, is one type of assured tenancy, and is for a fixed term of six months minimum and can be ended with two months' notice by serving a Form 6 Notice (S21 of the Housing Act 1988) notice (see below). Note that from 1st October 2018, Form 6A has replaced section 21 Notices for all tenancies where applicable.

It is important to note that all tenancies signed after February 1997 are assured shorthold agreements unless otherwise stated.

Assured tenancies are governed by the 1988 Housing Act, as amended by the 1996 Housing Act. It is to these Acts, or outlines of the Acts that the tenant must refer when intending to sign a tenancy for a residential property.

For a tenancy to be assured, three conditions must be fulfilled:
1. The premises must be a dwelling house. This basically means any

premises which can be lived in. Business premises will normally fall outside this interpretation.

2. There must exist a particular relationship between landlord and tenant. In other words, there must exist a tenancy agreement. For   example, a license to occupy, as in the case of students, or accommodation occupied because of work, cannot be seen as a tenancy. Following on from this, the accommodation must be let as a single unit. The tenant, who must be an individual, must normally be able to sleep, cook and eat in the accommodation. Sharing of bathroom facilities will not prevent a tenancy being an assured tenancy but shared cooking or other facilities, such as a living room, will.

3. The third requirement for an assured tenancy is that the tenant must occupy the dwelling as his or her only or principal home. In situations involving joint tenants at least one of them must occupy.

Tenancies that are not assured

A tenancy agreement will not be assured if one of the following conditions applies:

-The tenancy or the contract was entered into before 15th January 1989.

-If no rent is payable or if only a low rent amounting to less than two thirds of the present ratable value of the property is payable.

-If the premises are let for business purposes or for mixed residential and business purposes.

-If part of the dwelling house is licensed for the sale of liquor for consumption on the premises. This does not include the publican who lets out a flat.

-If the dwelling house is let with more than two acres of agricultural land.

-If the dwelling house is part of an agricultural holding and is occupied in relation to carrying out work on the holding.

-If the premises are let by a specified institution to students, i.e., halls of residence.

-If the premises are let for the purpose of a holiday.

-Where there is a resident landlord, e.g., in the case where the landlord has let one of his rooms but continues to live in the house.

-If the landlord is the Crown (the monarchy) or a government department. Certain lettings by the Crown are capable of being assured, such as some lettings by the Crown Estate Commissioners.

-If the landlord is a local authority, a fully mutual housing association (this is where you must be a shareholder to be a tenant) a newly created Housing Action Trust or any similar body listed in the 1988 Housing Act.

-If the letting is transitional such as a tenancy continuing in its original form until phased out, such as:

-A protected tenancy under the 1977 Rent Act.

-Secure tenancy granted before 1st January 1989, e.g., from a local authority or housing association. These tenancies are governed by the 1985 Housing Act).

The Assured Shorthold tenancy
The assured shorthold tenancy as we have seen, is the most common form of tenancy used in the private sector. The main principle of the assured shorthold tenancy is that it is issued for a period of six months minimum and can be ended by the landlord serving two-months notice on the tenant (Section 21 notice now replaced by Form 6A).

New rules for Section 21 notices

If the tenancy started or was renewed on or after 1 October 2015 a landlord needed to use the new prescribed Section 21 notice Form (6a). From 1st October 2018 landlords will now be required to use only Form 6A regardless of the start date.

Form 6A pre-requisites

A landlord cannot serve a valid Form 6A notice if:

- They have taken a deposit and not protected and/or served the prescribed information and/or
- They have failed to obtain a license for an HMO property which requires one

If the tenancy was in England and started or was renewed on or after 1 October 2015 a landlord must also have served on their tenant:

- an EPC (except where the property isn't required to have one)
- a Gas Safety Certificate, and
- the latest version of the Government's "How to Rent" Guide.
- Which scheme their deposit is protected in
- If the property is licensed a copy of the licence must be given to all licensees.

Plus, a landlord cannot serve a Form 6A notice if their Local Authority has served one of 3 specified notices (the most important being an improvement notice) on them within the past six months in respect of the poor condition of the rental property. Also, if the tenant complained about the issues covered by the notice prior to this – any

Form 6A notice served since the complaint and before the Local Authority notice was served will also be invalid.

The notice period must not be less than two months and must not end before the end of the fixed term (if this has not ended at the time the landlord served their notice)

If this is a periodic tenancy where the period (rent payment period) is more than monthly (e.g., a quarterly or six-month periodic tenancy), then the notice period must be at least one full tenancy period.

The notice period does not have to end on a particular day in the month, as was required under the old rules – the landlord just needs to make sure that the notice period is sufficient – minimum of 2 months.

Conditions for an assured shorthold tenancy

Any property let on an assured tenancy can be let on an assured shorthold, providing the following three conditions are met:

- The tenancy must be for a fixed term of not less than six months.
- The agreement cannot contain powers which enable the landlord to end the tenancy before six months. This does not include the right of the landlord to enforce the grounds for possession, which will be approximately the same as those for the assured tenancy
- A notice must be served before any rent increase giving one month's clear notice and providing details of the rent increase.

If the landlord wishes to get possession of his/her property, in this case before the expiry of the contractual term, the landlord must gain a court order. A notice of seeking possession (Form 6A previously s8 notice) must be served, giving fourteen days' notice, and following similar grounds of possession as an assured tenancy. *The landlord cannot simply tell a tenant to leave before the end of the agreed term.*

If the tenancy runs on after the end of the fixed term, then the landlord can regain possession by giving the required two months notice, as mentioned above.

At the end of the term for which the assured shorthold tenancy has been granted, the landlord has an automatic right to possession.

An assured shorthold tenancy will become periodic (will run from week to week) when the initial term of six months has elapsed, and the landlord has not brought the tenancy to an end. A periodic tenancy is ended with two months' notice. Assured shorthold tenants can be evicted only on certain grounds, some discretionary, some mandatory (see below).

For the landlord of an assured shorthold tenant to regain possession of the property, a notice of seeking possession (of property) must be served, giving fourteen days' notice of expiry, and stating the ground for possession. A copy of this notice is shown in Appendix 2.

Following the fourteen days a court order must be obtained. Although gaining a court order is not complicated, a solicitor will usually be used. Court costs can be awarded against the tenant.

Security of tenure: The ways in which a tenant can lose their home as an assured shorthold tenant

There are several circumstances called grounds (mandatory and discretionary) whereby a landlord can start a court action to evict a tenant.

The following are the *mandatory* grounds (where the judge must give the landlord possession) and *discretionary* grounds (where the

56

judge does not have to give the landlord possession) on which a court can order possession if the home is subject to an assured tenancy.

Mandatory grounds for possession of a property let on an assured (shorthold) tenancy

There are eight mandatory grounds for possession, which, if proved, leave the court with no choice but to make an order for possession. It is very important that you understand these.

Ground One is used where the landlord has served a notice, no later than at the beginning of the tenancy, warning the tenant that this ground may be used against him/her. This ground is used where the landlord wishes to recover the property as his or her principal (first and only) home or the spouse's (wife's or husbands) principal home.

The ground is not available to a person who bought the premises for gain (profit) whilst they were occupied.

Ground Two is available where the property is subject to a mortgage and if the landlord does not pay the mortgage, could lose the home.
Grounds Three and Four relate to holiday lettings.
Ground Five is a special one, applicable to ministers of religion.
Ground Six relates to the demolition or reconstruction of the property.
Ground Seven applies if a tenant dies and, in his will, leaves the tenancy to someone else: but the landlord must start proceedings against the new tenant within a year of the death if he wants to evict the new tenant.
Ground Eight concerns rent arrears. This ground applies if, both at the date of the serving of the notice seeking possession and at the date of the hearing of the action, the rent is at least 8 weeks in arrears or two

months in arrears. This is the main ground used by landlords when rent is not being paid.

The discretionary grounds for possession of a property, which is let on an assured tenancy

As we have seen, the discretionary grounds for possession are those in relation to which the court has some powers over whether the landlord can evict. In other words, the final decision is left to the judge. Often the judge will prefer to grant a suspended order first unless the circumstances are dramatic.

Ground Nine applies when suitable alternative accommodation is available or will be when the possession order takes effect. As we have seen, if the landlord wishes to obtain possession of his or her property to use it for other purposes then suitable alternative accommodation has to be provided.

Ground Ten deals with rent arrears as does *ground eleven*. These grounds are distinct from the mandatory grounds, as there does not have to be a fixed arrear in terms of time scale, e.g., 8 weeks. The judge, therefore, has some choice as to whether to evict. In practice, this ground will not be relevant to managers of assured shorthold tenancies.

Ground Twelve concerns any broken obligation of the tenancy. As we have seen with the protected tenancy, there are several conditions of the tenancy agreement, such as the requirement not to harass a neighbor racially or sexually. Ground Twelve will be used if these conditions are broken.

Ground Thirteen deals with the deterioration of the dwelling because of a tenant's neglect. This relates to the structure of the property and is the same as for a protected tenancy. It puts the responsibility on the tenant to look after the premises.

Ground Fourteen concerns nuisance, annoyance and illegal or immoral use. This is where a tenant or anyone connected with the tenant has caused a nuisance to neighbors.

Ground 14A this ground deals with domestic violence.

Ground 15 concerns the condition of the furniture and tenant's neglect. As Ground thirteen puts some responsibility on the tenant to look after the structure of the building so Ground Fifteen makes the tenant responsible for the furniture and fittings.

Ground 16 covers former employees. The premises were let to a former tenant by a landlord seeking possession and the tenant has ceased to be in that employment.

Ground 17 is where a person or that person's agents makes a false or reckless statement and this has caused the landlord to grant the tenancy under false pretences.

The description of the grounds above is intended as a guide only. A fuller description is contained within the 1988 Housing Act, section 7, Schedule two,) as amended by the 1996 Housing Act) which is available at reference libraries.

Fast track possession

In November 1993, following changes to the County Court Rules, a facility was introduced which enabled landlords of tenants with assured shorthold tenancies to apply for possession of their property without the usual time delay involved in waiting for a court date and attendance at court. This is known as "fast track possession" It cannot be used for rent arrears or other grounds. It is used to gain possession of a property when the fixed term of six months or more has come to an end and the tenant will not move.

Payment of rent

If the landlord wishes to raise rent, at least one month's minimum notice must be given. The rent cannot be raised more than once for the same tenant in one year. Tenants have the right to challenge a rent increase if they think it is unfair by referring the rent to a Rent Assessment Committee. The committee will prevent the landlord from raising the rent above the ordinary market rent for that type of property. We will be discussing rent and rent control further on in this book.

****

Chapter 5

JOINT TENANCIES

Although it is the normal situation for a tenancy agreement to be granted to one person, this is not always the case.

A tenancy can also be granted to two or more people and is then known as a *joint tenancy*. The position of joint tenants is the same as that of single tenants. In other words, there is still one tenancy even though it is shared. Each tenant is responsible for paying the rent and observing the terms and conditions of the tenancy agreement. No one joint tenant can prevent another joint tenant's access to the premises. If one of the joint tenants dies, then his or her interest will automatically pass to the remaining joint tenants. A joint tenant cannot dispose of his or her interest in a will.

Joint tenants usually all have the same rights and responsibilities in their rented home and are all responsible for paying the rent.

Joint Tenancy agreements
You have a joint tenancy if you and your flatmates or housemates all signed a single tenancy agreement with a landlord when you moved in. This means that you all have the same rights and responsibilities. If each of you signed a separate agreement with the landlord, you have separate tenancies.

Rent liability when you're a joint tenant

Joint tenants are all jointly and individually responsible for paying the rent. This means that if one of you moves out without giving notice or is not paying their share, the other joint tenants are responsible for paying it for them. If none of you pay your rent, your landlord can ask any one of you to pay the full amount. All the joint tenants are usually also responsible for paying gas and electricity bills.

Tenancy deposits

When you move into private rented accommodation, you usually need to pay a deposit to cover any damage or unpaid rent. Pay the deposit directly to the landlord or letting agency. If you have an assured shorthold tenancy check that your deposit is put into a tenancy deposit scheme.

Deductions from a tenancy deposit

The landlord normally takes a single deposit for the whole of the tenancy. If one joint tenant fails to pay their share of the rent or if they cause damage to the property, the landlord is entitled to deduct the shortfall or damage from the deposit. You and the other joint tenants decide how to divide up the remaining deposit when it is returned.

Tenancy deposits when a joint tenant moves out

If you are replacing another tenant who is moving out, they may ask you to pay the deposit to them instead. This may not be a good idea. If the tenant who is moving out has caused any damage to the property or left any unpaid bills, the landlord can deduct these costs from the deposit when you move out, which could leave you out of pocket. Get advice if you are in this situation. It might be better to ask the landlord to give a new tenancy agreement to the tenants who is staying on.

Permission for changes
You need to get written permission from the other joint tenants if you want to carry out improvements to the property or pass on or assign your tenancy to someone else. In most cases you also need your landlord's permission to do any of these things, or if you want to take in a lodger.

Ending a joint tenancy: when one person leaves
The rules on how and when a tenancy can be ended depend on whether the tenancy is fixed term (for a set period) or periodic (rolling from week to week or month to month). See the section on ending a tenancy for more information. If you want to leave, discuss this with the other joint tenants before you take any action. A fixed-term tenancy cannot be ended early unless all the joint tenants agree and either:

- your landlord agrees that the tenancy can end early (this is called a 'surrender'), or
- there is a 'break clause' in your tenancy agreement, which allows you to give notice and leave early

If you have a periodic tenancy, or the fixed term has ended and your tenancy has not been renewed, one tenant can end the whole tenancy and does not need the agreement of the other joint tenants. The landlord must be given a valid written notice and there are special rules about how and when this must be done.

Leaving a joint tenancy
If you want to leave a joint tenancy, it is usually best to discuss it with the other joint tenants before you take any action. If the other joint

tenant(s) don't want to move out, they can try to negotiate a new agreement with the landlord. The remaining tenants may be able to find another person to take on the tenancy of the person who wants to leave (the landlord would have to agree to this) or agree with the other joint tenants to stay on and pay the extra rent themselves. Your landlord may decide to:

- Give the other tenants a new tenancy agreement, listing the new tenants (in practice, your landlord might not bother to do this)
- accept the rent from the new tenant – in which case the new tenant should have the same rights as a tenant whose name is on the tenancy agreement

Eviction of joint tenants

Your landlord cannot evict one joint tenant without evicting all the others. Instead, your landlord may be able to end the tenancy (using the procedures for eviction) and offer a new one to the remaining tenants. Talk to your landlord as soon as possible if you are in this situation and you want to stay.

Relationship breakdown

Get advice if you are worried about losing your home after a relationship breakdown. You may have rights that you are not aware of. For example:

- it may be possible for your joint tenancy to be transferred into one person's name – this can sometimes be done even if the other joint tenant won't agree to it
- it may be possible to stop the other joint tenant from ending the tenancy by applying for an occupation order or an injunction

Problems with joint tenancies

If you have a problem with another joint tenant, you probably have to sort these out yourself. Landlords are usually reluctant to get involved, although council or housing associations are more likely to get involved than private landlords.

****

Chapter 6

THE RIGHT TO QUIET ENJOYMENT OF A HOME

Earlier, we saw that when a tenancy agreement is signed, the landlord is contracting to give quiet enjoyment of the tenant's home. This means that they have the right to live peacefully in the home without harassment.

The landlord is obliged not to do anything that will disturb the right to the quiet enjoyment of the home. The most serious breach of this right would be for the landlord to wrongfully evict a tenant.

Eviction: what can be done against unlawful harassment and eviction
It is a criminal offence for a landlord unlawfully to evict a residential occupier (whether or not a tenant!). The occupier has protection under the Protection from Eviction Act 1977 section 1(2). In addition, there is protection under the Human Rights Act. For advice on the law in Northern Ireland go to: www.housingadviceni.org. For Scotland go to: scotland.shelter.org.uk

If the tenant or occupier is unlawfully evicted his/her first course should be to seek an injunction compelling the landlord to readmit him/her to the premises. It is an unfortunate fact, but many landlords will attempt to evict tenants forcefully. In doing so they break the law.

However, the landlord may, on termination of the tenancy recover possession without a court order if the agreement was entered into after 15th January 1989 and it falls into one of the following six situations:

- The occupier shares any accommodation with the landlord and the landlord occupies the premises as his or her only or principal home.
- The occupier shares any of the accommodation with a member of the landlord's family, that person occupies the premises as their only or principal home, and the landlord occupies as his or her only or principal home premises in the same building.
- The tenancy or license was granted temporarily to an occupier who entered the premises as a trespasser.
- The tenancy or license gives the right to occupy for the purposes of a holiday.
- The tenancy or license is rent-free.
- The license relates to occupation of a hostel.

There is also a section in the 1977 Protection from Eviction Act which provides a defense for otherwise unlawful eviction and that is that the landlord may repossess if it is thought that the tenant no longer lives on the premises. It is important to note that, for such action to be seen as a crime under the 1977 Protection from Eviction Act, the intention of the landlord to evict must be proved. However, there is another offence, namely harassment, which also needs to be proved. Even if the landlord is not guilty of permanently depriving a tenant of their home, he/she could be guilty of harassment. Such actions as cutting off services, deliberately allowing the premises to fall into a state of disrepair, or even forcing unwanted sexual attentions, all constitute harassment and a breach of the right to *quiet enjoyment*.

The 1977 Protection from Eviction Act also prohibits the use of violence to gain entry to premises. Even in situations where the landlord has the right to gain entry without a court order it is an offence to use violence.

If entry to the premises is opposed, then the landlord should gain a court order.

What can be done against unlawful evictions?

There are two main remedies for unlawful eviction: damages and, as stated above, an injunction. An injunction is an order from the court requiring a person to do, or not to do something. In the case of eviction, the court can grant an injunction requiring the landlord to allow a tenant back into occupation of the premises. In the case of harassment an order can be made preventing the landlord from harassing the tenant. Failure to comply with an injunction is contempt of court and can result in a fine or imprisonment.

Damages

In some cases, the tenant can press for *financial compensation* following unlawful eviction. Financial compensation may have to be paid in cases where financial loss has occurred or in cases where personal hardship alone has occurred.

The tenant can also press for *special damages,* which means that the tenant may recover the definable out-of-pocket expenses. These could be expenses arising because of having to stay in a hotel because of the eviction. Receipts must be kept in that case. There are also *general damages*, which can be awarded in compensation for stress, suffering and inconvenience.

A tenant may also seek *exemplary damages* where it can be proved that the landlord has disregarded the law deliberately with the intention of making a profit out of the displacement of the tenant.

Chapter 7

LANDLORD AND TENANT REPAIRING OBLIGATIONS

Repairs and improvements generally: The landlord and tenants' obligations

Repairs are essential works to keep the property in good order. Improvements and alterations to the property, e.g., the installation of a shower. (See summary of disrepair cases at the end of the chapter). Repairing obligations have been difficult to carry out during the pandemic but have eased somewhat in 2022. For more advice on COVID and repairs go:

https://england.shelter.org.uk/housing_advice/coronavirus

As we have seen, most tenancies are periodic, i.e., week-to-week or month-to-month. If a tenancy falls into this category or is a fixed-term tenancy for less than seven years, and began after October 1961, then a landlord is legally responsible for most major repairs to the flat or house.

If a tenancy began after 15th January 1989, then, in addition to the above responsibility, the landlord is also responsible for repairs to common parts and service fittings.

The area of law dealing with the landlord and tenants repairing obligations is the 1985 Landlord and Tenant Act, section 11.

This section of the Act is known as a covenant and cannot be excluded by informal agreement between landlord and tenant. In other words, the landlord is legally responsible whether he or she likes it or not. Parties to a tenancy, however, may make an application to a court mutually to vary or exclude this section.

Example of repairs a landlord is responsible for:
- Leaking roofs and guttering.
- Rotting windows.
- Rising damp.
- Damp walls.
- Faulty electrical wiring.
- Dangerous ceilings and staircases.
- Faulty gas and water pipes.
- Broken water heaters and boilers.
- Broken lavatories, sinks or baths.

In shared housing the landlord must see that shared halls, stairways, kitchens, and bathrooms are maintained and kept clean and lit.

Normally, tenants are responsible only for minor repairs, e.g., broken door handles, cupboard doors, etc. Tenants will also be responsible for decorations unless they have been damaged because of the landlord's failure to do repair.

A landlord will be responsible for repairs only if the repair has been reported. It is therefore important to report repairs in writing and keep a copy. If the repair is not carried out, then action can be taken. Damages can also be claimed. Compensation can be claimed, with the appropriate amount being the reduction in the value of the premises to the tenant caused by the landlord's failure to repair. If the tenant carries out the repairs, then the amount expended will represent the decrease in value. The tenant does not have the right to withhold rent because of a breach of repairing covenant by the landlord. However, depending on the repair, the landlord will not have a very strong case in court if rent is withheld.

Reporting repairs to landlords

The tenant must tell the landlord or the person collecting the rent straight away when a repair needs doing. It is advisable that it is in writing, listing the repairs that need to be done. Once a tenant has reported a repair the landlord must do it within a reasonable period. What is reasonable will depend on the nature of the repair.

The tenants' rights whilst repairs are being carried out

The landlord must ensure that the repairs are done in an orderly and efficient way with minimum inconvenience to the tenant If the works are disruptive or if property or decorations are damaged the tenant can apply to the court for compensation or, if necessary, for an order to make the landlord behave reasonably. If the landlord genuinely needs the house empty to do the work, he/she can ask the tenant to vacate it and can if necessary, get a court order against the tenant.

A written agreement should be drawn up making it clear that the tenant can move back in when the repairs are completed and stating what the arrangements for fuel charges and rent are.

Can the landlord put the rent up after doing repairs?

If there is a service charge for maintenance, the landlord may be able to pass on the cost of the work(s).

Tenants' rights to make improvements to a property

Unlike carrying out repairs the tenant will not normally have the right to insist that the landlord make actual alterations to the home.

However, a tenant needs the following amenities and the law states that you should have:

- Bath or shower.
- Wash hand basin.
- Hot and cold water at each bath, basin, or shower.
- An indoor toilet.

If these amenities do not exist, then the tenant can contact the council's Environmental Health Officer. An improvement notice can be served on the landlord ordering him to put the amenity in.

Disabled tenants

If a tenant is disabled, he/she may need special items of equipment in the accommodation. The local authority may help in providing and, occasionally, paying for these. The tenant will need to obtain the permission of the landlord. If you require more information, then contact the social services department locally.

Houses in multiple occupation (HMO)

A landlord has extra legal responsibilities if the house or flat shared with other tenants is a house in multiple occupation (HMO). The extra rules are there to reduce the risk of fire and to make sure that people living in shared houses or flats have adequate facilities. From 1st October 2018, all landlords who fall within the HMO category must be licensed by the local authority for the area.

A home is an HMO if:

- 3 or more unrelated people live there as at least 2 separate households – for example, 3 single people with their own rooms, or 2 couples each sharing a room the 3 or more people living there share basic amenities, such as a kitchen or bathroom. The requirement for the property to cover three or more stories of a property has now been removed and it is estimated that this change will mean that some 177,000 rental properties will now be classed as HMOs.

A home is a large HMO if both of the following apply:
- at least 5 tenants live there, forming more than 1 household
- They share toilet, bathroom, or kitchen facilities with other tenants
- A household is either a single person or members of the same family who live together. A family includes people who are:
- married or living together - including people in same-sex relationships
- relatives or half-relatives, for example grandparents, aunts, uncles, siblings
- stepparents and stepchildren

An HMO could be a:
- house split into separate bedsits
- shared house or flat, where the sharers are not members of the same family
- hostel
- bed-and-breakfast hotel that is not just for holidays
- shared accommodation for students – although many halls of residence and other types of student accommodation owned by educational establishments are not classed as HMOs

Extra responsibilities of HMO landlords

Landlords of HMOs must make sure that:

- proper fire safety measures are in place, including working smoke alarms
- annual gas safety checks are carried out
- electrics are checked every 5 years
- the property is not overcrowded
- there are enough cooking and bathroom facilities for the number living there
- communal areas and shared facilities are clean and in good repair
- there are enough rubbish bins/bags

Responsibility for repairs in HMOs

A landlord is responsible for any repairs to communal areas of A home. They are also responsible for repairs to:

- the structure and exterior of the house – including the walls, window frames and gutters
- water and gas pipes
- electrical wiring
- basins, sinks, baths, and toilets
- fixed heaters (radiators) and water heaters

HMOs don't need to be licensed if they are managed or owned by a housing association or co-operative, a council, a health service or a police or fire authority.

Licences usually last for 5 years but some councils grant them for shorter periods. When deciding whether to issue or renew a licence, the council checks that:

- the property meets an acceptable standard. For example, it looks at whether the property is large enough for the occupants and if it is well managed
- the landlord is a 'fit and proper' person
- Minimum bedroom size for HMOs

If a landlord applied for a HMO licence on or after 1 October 2018 or has renewed it since, bedroom sizes must be at least:

6.51 square metres for an adult
10.22 square metres for two adults
4.64 square metres for a child under 10 years old

Some councils may set higher standards for bedroom sizes.
If a room is used as bedroom and doesn't meet the size requirement, the council may allow a landlord up to 18 months to make the room larger or move you to a different bedroom. The council can prosecute or fine a landlord if a bedroom is smaller than standards allow.

Landlord penalties for not having an HMO licence
A landlord can be fined and ordered to repay up to 12 months' rent if tenants live in a HMO that should be licensed but isn't. A tenants can apply for a rent repayment order within a year of the HMO being unlicensed, and any housing benefit or universal credit tenants have used to help them pay rent will be reclaimed by the council.

The council can prosecute landlords of HMOs, or any manager they have employed, if they break the law. In extreme cases, the council can take over the management of the property.

Safety generally for all landlords-the regulations

The main product safety regulations relevant to the lettings industry are:

Gas safety

The Gas safety (Installation and use) Regulations 1998
The Gas Cooking Appliances (safety) Regulations 1989
Heating Appliances (Fireguard) (safety) Regulations 1991
Gas Appliances (Safety) Regulations 1995

All the above are because the supply of gas and the appliances in a dwelling must be safe. A Gas Safety certificate is required to validate this.

Furniture Safety

Furniture and Furnishings (Fire) (Safety) Regulations 1988 and 1993 (as amended). Landlords and lettings agents are included in these regulations. The regulations set high standards for fire resistance for domestic upholstered furniture and other products containing upholstery.

The Regulations apply to any upholstered furniture manufactured after 1st January 1950 intended for use in a dwelling including:

- All types of upholstered seating including chairs, settees, padded stools, and ottomans. Children's furniture, foot stools, sofa-beds, futons and other convertibles, bean bags and floor cushions nursery furniture and upholstered items designed to contain a baby or small child. Domestic upholstered furniture that is supplied in kit form for self-assembly. Second hand furniture Upholstered headboards, footboards, and side rails of beds.

- Furniture for use in the open air (garden and outdoor furniture) which is suitable for use in a dwelling (homes or caravans) such as conservatory furniture
- Upholstery in caravans (although not vehicles or boats) and Cane furniture which includes upholstery.
- Divans, bed-bases, mattresses, pillows, and mattress pads (toppers) scatter cushions and seat pads (FILLING MATERIAL ONLY)
- Permanent covers for furniture (textiles, coated textiles, leather etc) Loose and stretch covers for furniture. Covers for non-visible parts of furniture
- Foam and non-foam filling material for furniture

What items are not covered?
- Upholstered furniture manufactured before 1st January 1950
- Materials used solely to recover pre--1950 furniture
- Sleeping Bags
- Bed Clothes or Duvets
- Loose Mattress Covers
- Pillowcases
- Curtains
- Carpets

Upholstered articles (i.e., beds, sofas, armchairs etc) must have fire resistant filling material.

Upholstered articles must have passed a match resistant test or, if of certain kinds (such as cotton or silk) be used with a fire resistant interliner.

The combination of the cover fabric and the filling material must have passed a cigarette resistance test.

The landlord should inspect property for non-compliant items before letting and replace with compliant items.

Electrical Safety
Electrical Equipment (Safety) Regulations 1994
Plugs and Sockets etc. (Safety) Regulations 1994.

Electrical hazards are also covered by the Housing Health and safety Rating System under the Housing Act 2004. In the case of commercial property and houses in multiple occupation there is a statutory duty under the Regulatory Reform Fire Safety Order 2005 for the responsible person (the property manager) to carry out annual Fire Safety Risk Assessments, which include electrical safety risks.

The Electrical Equipment Regulations came into force in January 1995. Both sets of regulations relate to the supply of electrical equipment designed with a working voltage of between 50- and 1000-volts ac. (or between 75- and 1000-volts dc.) the regulations cover all the mains voltage household electrical goods including cookers, kettles, toasters, electric blankets, washing machines, immersion heaters etc. The regulations do not apply to items attached to land. This is generally considered to exclude the fixed wiring and built-in appliances (e.g. central heating systems) from the regulations. Lettings agents and landlords should take the following action:

Essential:
Check all electrical appliances in all managed properties on a regular fixed term basis. Remove unsafe items and keep a record of checks.

Recommended:

- Have appliances checked by a qualified electrical engineer
- Avoid purchasing second hand electrical items
- There is no specific requirement for regular testing under the regulations. However, it is recommended that a schedule of checks, say on an annual basis, is put in place.

For more information on electrical safety visit: www.landlordzone.co.uk/information/electrical-safety. This is a particularly good site.

Tougher rules announced for electrical inspections for rented homes in the UK (January 2019 and January 2020)

Rules on electrical safety in the UK's private rented sector have been tightened to ensure mandatory electrical checks are carried out by competent and qualified inspectors.

The tougher rules mean greater protection for tenants and help drive up standards in the lettings sector.

Landlords are legally required to ensure that the inspectors they hire to carry out safety inspections have the necessary competence and qualifications to do so with tough financial penalties for those who fail to comply.

Ministers will also publish new guidance which sets out the minimum level of competence and qualifications necessary for those carrying out these important inspections, meaning both landlords and tenants can be assured their home is safe from electrical faults.

On the 13th of January 2020, a full detailed set of regulations were laid out before parliament for their consideration. The "Electrical Safety Standards in the Private Rented Sector (England) Regulations

2020" detail the new requirements for electrical safety checks in rental properties and the expected timescales for their implementation.

In a nutshell, the regulations require that every private rented property has an electrical inspection completed by a suitably qualified person, a minimum of every 5 years.

There are instances where this timescale may be shorter, such as where the previous inspection has suggested a shorter timeframe due to the condition of the installation. The implementation of the new regulations will be as follows:

- New Tenancies - New tenancies must meet the new requirements from July 1st, 2020
- **Existing Tenancies** - Existing tenancies must meet the new requirements from April 1st, 2021

The regulations also require that:

- Landlords provide a copy of the electrical inspection report to the tenant within 28 days of the inspection (or before the tenancy begins for new tenants)
- Landlords must supply a copy to the local authority within 7 days (if requested to do so)
- Any faults highlighted by the electrical inspection must be remedied within 28 days (or sooner if detailed within the electrical report)
- Written confirmation must be obtained to confirm that any necessary repairs have been completed

Non-compliance with the new regulations will mean the local authority will supply the landlord with an 'enforcement notice'. If a landlord fails to act upon this, the local authority can enforce it by having the repairs completed (and billing the landlord) or even impose a fine of up to £30,000

The availability of grants

There are several grants available to landlords at any one time which will enable improvements to take place to a property. One of the main grants is the Disabled facilities Grant. However, there are more, and your local authority can tell you what is available.

Regulations on Smoke and Carbon Monoxide detectors

From October 2015, all landlords, regardless of whether public or private sector, are required to install working smoke and carbon monoxide alarms in their properties, on each floor. The carbon monoxide alarms need to be placed in high-risk areas, i.e., where there are gas appliances such as boilers or fires. Carbon monoxide detectors will not be required in properties where there are no gas or solid fuel appliances.

A civil penalty of up to £5,000 will apply to landlords who fail to comply with this legislation.

Obligations on Landlords to upgrade and maintain insulation

From April 2018, properties rented out in the private rented sector are required to have a minimum energy performance rating of E. The regulations will apply to new lets and renewals of tenancies and will apply to all existing tenancies from 1st April 2020. It will be against the law to rent a property which has a rating lower than E unless there is an applicable exemption.

Legionnaire's disease

It is the responsibility of all landlords to undertake a risk assessment to prevent the spread of the Legionella bacteria, which can be found in a property's water systems and can lead to Legionnaires' disease if inhaled.

Legionnaires' disease is a pneumonia-like illness caused by Legionella bacteria and can be fatal. It is one of several conditions included within the Legionellosis group. Although the risks are generally very low in residential property, health and safety legislation in the UK requires landlords to carry out risk assessments to control the exposure to tenants of Legionella.

The risk of Legionnaires' disease is likely to be higher in properties that are left empty and where water may be left to stand in both hot and cold systems, thus increasing the opportunity for the bacteria to multiply in the standing water. As such, it is vital landlords ensure water systems are used at least once a week. And if a property is set to remain empty for several months, it may be worth draining the system to prevent the possibility of bacteria developing to unacceptable levels.

To minimise or eliminate the risk posed by Legionella, landlords should:

• Maintain cold water below 20 degrees C, as Legionella thrives in water between 20 and 45 degrees C
• Ensure showers and taps that are used infrequently - such as those in spare bedrooms - are periodically flushed through with running water•
Cover water tanks so mice, birds, insects, and other creatures cannot gain access
• Remove unnecessary pipes, such as those leading to appliances that are no longer used

Signs of Legionella include:

- Cold water running warm
- Water that is discoloured or contains debris
- A malfunctioning boiler or hot water system

Sanitation health and hygiene generally

Local authorities have a duty to serve an owner with a notice requiring the provision of a WC when a property has insufficient sanitation, sanitation meaning toilet waste disposal.

They will also serve notice if it is thought that the existing sanitation is inadequate and is harmful to health or is a nuisance.

Local authorities have similar powers under various Public Health Acts to require owners to put right bad drains and sewers, also food storage facilities and vermin, plus the containing of disease.

The Environmental Health Department, if it considers the problem bad enough will serve a notice requiring the landlord to put the defect right. In certain cases, the local authority can do the work and require the landlord to pay for it. This is called work in default.

****

Chapter 8

TAKING BACK POSSESSION OF A PROPERTY

The Coronavirus Act 2020 and its temporary limitations on serving notice and evictions has been relaxed. Landlords can now act to repossess property The below is a summary of the situation which now exists.

Fast-track possession

A landlord cannot serve a s21 notice (Form 6A) on an assured shorthold tenant until after the first four months of a tenancy (if it is for a six-month period). This brings the tenancy to an end on the day of expiry, i.e., on the day of expiry of the six-month period,

Rules for Section 21 notices

If the tenancy started or was renewed on or after 1 October 2015 a landlord will need to use the new prescribed Section 21 notice Form (6a). Form 6A has replaced both S21 and S8 Notices although the Form still relates to S21 and S6 of the Housing Act.

Section 21 (Form 6A) pre-requisites

A landlord cannot serve a valid Form 6A notice if:
- They have taken a deposit and not protected and/or served the prescribed information and/or
- They have failed to obtain a license for an HMO property which requires one

If the tenancy was in England and started or was renewed on or after 1 October 2015 a landlord must also have served on their tenant (and you should get proof of service for all these:

- an EPC
- a Gas Safety Certificate, and
- the latest version of the Government's "How to Rent" Guide.
- Which deposit scheme the tenants deposit is in

Plus, a landlord cannot serve a section 21 notice if their Local Authority has served one of 3 specified notices (the most important being an improvement notice) on them within the past six months in respect of the poor condition of the rental property.

Also, if the tenant complained about the issues covered by the notice prior to this – any Section 21 notice served since the complaint and before the Local Authority notice was served will also be invalid.

The notice period must not be less than two months and must not end before the end of the fixed term (if this has not ended at the time the landlord served their notice)

If this is a periodic tenancy where the period (rent payment period) is more than monthly (e.g., a quarterly or six-month periodic tenancy), then the notice period must be at least one full tenancy period.

The notice period does not have to end on a particular day in the month, as was required under the old rules – the landlord just needs to make sure that the notice period is sufficient – minimum of 2 months.

On expiry of the notice, if it is the landlord's intention to take possession of the property then the tenants should leave. It is worthwhile writing a letter to the tenants one month before expiry reminding them that they should leave. In the event of the tenant refusing to leave, then the landlord must then follow a process termed 'fast track possession'. This entails filling in the appropriate forms (N5B) which can be downloaded from Her Majesty's Court Service Website www.justice.gov.uk.

Assuming that a valid Form 6A notice has been served on the tenant, the accelerated possession proceedings can begin, and the forms completed and lodged with the court dealing with the area where the property is situated. To grant the accelerated possession order the court will require the following:

- The assured shorthold agreement
- The section 21 notice (Form 6A)
- Evidence of service of the notice

The best form of service of the Form 6A notice is by hand. If you have already served the notice, then evidence that the tenant has received it will be required. Having the correct original paperwork is of the utmost importance. Without this, the application will fail, and delays will be incurred.

If the tenant disputes the possession proceedings in any way, they will have 14 days to reply to the court. If the case is well founded and the paperwork is in order, then there should be no case for defence. Once the accelerated possession order has been granted then this will need to be served on the tenant, giving them 14 days to vacate. In certain circumstances, if the tenant pleads hardship the court can grant extra time to leave, six weeks as opposed to two weeks. If they still do not vacate, then an application will need to be made to court for a bailiffs warrant to evict the tenants.

Accelerated possession proceedings cannot be used against the tenant for rent arrears. It will be necessary to follow the procedure below.

An accelerated possession order remains in force for six years from the date it was granted.

Going to court to end the tenancy

There may come a time when a landlord needs to go to court to regain possession of their property. This will usually arise when the contract has been breached by the tenant, for non-payment of rent or for some other breach such as nuisance or harassment. As we have seen, a tenancy can be ended in a court on one of the grounds for possession. However, as the tenancy will usually be an assured shorthold then it is necessary to consider for the landlord to consider whether they are able to give two months notice and withhold the deposit, as opposed to going to court. The act of withholding the deposit will entail the landlord refusing to authorize the payment to the tenant online. This then brings arbitration into the frame. Deposit schemes have an arbitration system as an integral part of the scheme.

If a landlord decides, for whatever reason, to go to court, then any move to regain a property for breach of agreement will commence in the county court in the area in which the property is. The first steps in ending the tenancy will necessitate the serving of a notice of seeking possession Form 6A using one of the Grounds for Possession detailed earlier in the book. If the tenancy is protected then 28 days must be given, the notice must be in prescribed form and served on the tenant personally (preferably).

If the tenancy is an assured shorthold, which is more often the case now, then 14 days notice of seeking possession can be used. In all cases the ground to be relied upon must be clearly outlined in the notice. If the case is more complex, then this will entail a particulars of claim being prepared, usually by a solicitor, as opposed to a standard possession form.

A fee is paid when sending the particulars to court, which should be checked with the local county court. The standard form which the landlord uses for routine rent arrears cases is called the N119 and the accompanying summons is called the N5. Both forms can be obtained from the court or from www.courtservice.gov. When completed, the forms should be sent in duplicate to the county court and a copy retained for you.

•The court will send a copy of the particulars of claim and the summons to the tenant. They will send the landlord a form which gives them a case number and court date to appear, known as the return date. On the return date, the landlord should arrive at court at least 15 minutes early. Complainants can represent themselves in simple cases but are advised to use a solicitor for more contentious cases.

If the tenant is present, then they will have a chance to defend themselves.

Several orders are available. However, if you a person has gone to court on the mandatory ground eight then if the fact is proved then they will get possession immediately. If not, then the judge can grant an order, suspended whilst the tenant finds time to pay.

In a lot of cases, it is more expedient for a landlord to serve notice-requiring possession, if the tenancy has reached the end of the period, and then wait two months before the property is regained. This saves the cost and time of going to court particularly if the ground is one of nuisance or other, which will involve solicitors.

In many cases, if landlords are contemplating going to court and have never been before and do not know the procedure then it is best to use a solicitor to guide the case through.

Costs can be recovered from the tenant, although this will depend on their means. If possession is regained midway through the contractual term, then the landlord will have to complete the possession process by use of bailiff, pay a fee and fill in another form, Warrant for Possession of Land.

If a landlord has reached the end of the contractual term and wish to recover their property, then a fast-track procedure is available which entails gaining an order for possession and bailiff's order by post. This can be used in cases except for rent arrears.

****

Chapter 9

PRIVATE TENANCIES IN SCOTLAND

The law governing the relationship between private landlords and tenants in Scotland is different to that in England. Since the beginning of 1989, new private sector tenancies in Scotland were covered by the Housing (Scotland) Act 1988. Following the passage of this Act, private sector tenants no longer had any protection as far as rent levels were concerned and tenants enjoyed less security of tenure. However, The **Private Housing (Tenancies) (Scotland) Act 2016**, passed by the Scottish Parliament and coming into force on 1st December 2017 has changed the law concerning private tenancies in Scotland. The main provisions of the Act are outlined below.

The new Private Residential Tenancy

On 1 December 2017 a new type of tenancy came into force, called the private residential tenancy, it replaced assured and short assured tenancy agreements for all new tenancies from 1st December 2017. because of passing of The Private Housing (Tenancies) (Scotland) Act 2016. The new Scottish Private Residential Tenancy, (SPRT) will deliver improved security of tenure for tenants, including students in smaller purpose built and mainstream private rented accommodation, and the power for local authorities to designate rent pressure zones within their jurisdiction. There will also be streamlined procedures for starting and ending a tenancy and a model agreement for landlords and tenants.

The SPRT will become the standard tenancy agreement between residential landlords and tenants and will replace the most common types of residential tenancies in Scotland – the Short-Assured Tenancy and the Assured Tenancy.

What changes has the private residential tenancy brought in?
Any tenancy that started on or after 1 December 2017 will be a private residential tenancy. These new tenancies will bring in changes and improvements to the private rented sector, including:

- **No more fixed terms** - private residential tenancies are open ended, meaning a landlord can't ask a tenant to leave just because they have been in the property for 6 months as they can with a short-assured tenancy.
- **Rent increases** – a tenant's rent can only be increased once every 12 months (with 3 months notice) and if they think the proposed increase is unfair, they can refer it to a rent officer.
- **Longer notice period** - if a tenant has lived in a property for longer than 6 months the landlord will have to give them at least 84 days notice to leave (unless they have broken a term in the tenancy).
- **Simpler notices** - the notice to quit process has been scrapped and replaced by a simpler notice to leave process.
- **Model tenancy agreement** - the Scottish Government have published a model private residential tenancy that can be used by landlords to set up a tenancy.

Person already an assured/short-assured tenant
If a tenant was already renting and were an assured or short assured tenant, on 1 December 2017, their tenancy will continue as normal until they or their landlord brings it to an end following the correct

procedure. If a landlord then offers a tenant a new tenancy this will be a private residential tenancy.

What is a private residential tenancy?
A private residential tenancy is one that meets the following conditions:

- the tenancy started on or after 1 December 2017
- it is let to a person as a separate dwelling (home)
- the person must be an individual, meaning not a company
- it's their main or only home
- they must have a lease (although a written agreement not needed for a lease to exist)
- the tenancy is not a exemptions tenancy, as listed below.

Tenancy agreements
A person has the right to a tenancy agreement, which can be either a written or electronic copy, within 28 days of the start of the tenancy. The Scottish Government has published a model tenancy that a landlord can use to set up a tenancy. This tenancy plus a set of notes that a landlord must give to the tenant can be accessed at www.mygov.scot/tenancy-agreement-scotland.

This tenancy agreement contains certain statutory terms that outline both party's rights and obligations including:

- The tenant's and landlord/letting agent's contact details
- The address and details of the rented property
- The start date of the tenancy
- How much the rent is and how it can be increased
- How much the deposit is and information about how it will be registered

- Who is responsible for insuring the property?
- The tenant must inform the landlord when they are going to be absent from the property for more than 14 days
- The tenant will take reasonable care of the property
- The condition that the landlord must make sure the property is in, including the repairing standard.
- That the tenant must inform the landlord the need of any repairs.
- That the tenant will give reasonable access to the property, when the landlord has given at least 48 hours notice
- The process that the tenancy can be ended

If a landlord uses the Scottish Government's' model tenancy, they should also give the tenant the 'Easy Read Notes' which will explain the tenancy terms in plain English. If a landlord does not use the model tenancy, they must give the tenant the private residential tenancy statutory terms: supporting notes, with their lease, which will explain the basic set of terms that a landlord has to include in the lease.

Rent Increases
The rent can only be increase once every 12 months and the landlord needs to give a tenant 3 months notice, using the correct notice of the rent increase. If the tenant doesn't agree to the rent increase, they can refer it to the local rent officer. The referral to the rent officer must be done within 21 days of receiving the rent increase notice.

When a referral made to the rent officer, they will first issue a provisional order which will suggest the amount the rent can be increased. The tenant will have 14 days from the date the provisional order is issued to request a reconsideration. If the tenant requests a reconsideration the rent officer will look at it again before making a final order and telling them the date that the increase will take place.

Ending a tenancy

If a tenant wants to end the tenancy, then they will have to give the landlord 28 days' notice in writing. The notice must state the day on which the tenancy is to end, normally the day after notice period has expired.

The tenant can agree a different notice period with the landlord as long it is in writing. If there is no agreed notice, then 28 days' notice is the minimum required.

Landlord access

The tenant must allow reasonable access to the landlord to carry out repairs, inspections, or valuations when:

* the landlord has given at least 48 hours' written notice, or
* access is required urgently for the landlord to view or carry out works in relation to the repairing standard

If a tenant refuses access the landlord can make an application to the First Tier Tribunal Housing and Property Chamber who may make an order allowing them access.

Getting repairs carried out

As with other tenancies, the landlord must keep the property wind and watertight, and in a condition that is safe to live in. The landlord is also responsible for making sure that the property repairing standard is met. This is a basic level of repair that is required by law. The landlord must give the tenant information on the repairing standard and what they can do if the property does not meet it. If a tenant wants to carry out work on their home, such as redecorating or installing a second phone line, they will need to seek permission from the landlord. Some tenancy agreements will include a clause telling the tenant whether they can carry out this kind of work.

Can a tenant sublet or pass their tenancy on to someone else?
A tenant cannot sublet, take in a lodger, or pass their tenancy on to someone else before first getting written agreement from the landlord.

Tenancies that cannot be private residential tenancy
Almost all new private tenancies created on or after 1st December 2017 will be private residential tenancies. However, there are several exemptions, including the following:

- Tenancies at a low rent
- Tenancies of shops
- Licensed premises
- Tenancies of agricultural land
- Lettings to students (meaning purpose-built student accommodation)
- Holiday lettings
- Resident landlords
- Police Housing
- Military Housing
- Social Housing
- Sublet, assigned etc. social housing
- Homeless persons
- Persons on probation or released from prison etc.
- Accommodation for asylum seekers
- Displaced persons

- Shared ownership
- Tenancies under previous legislation
- Assured or short assured tenancies

Short assured and assured tenancies

Most residential lettings in Scotland made after 2 January 1989 and before 1st December 2017 are short-assured tenancies. Those that - weren't short assured are normally assured tenancies.

Short assured tenancies

This was the most common type of tenancy. A short-assured tenancy makes it easier for a landlord to get a property than an assured tenancy. Before any agreement is signed, a landlord must use form AT5 to tell new tenants that the tenancy will be a short-assured tenancy. (See appendix). If they don't, the tenancy will automatically be an assured tenancy. Initially, a short-assured tenancy must be for 6 months or more. After the first 6 months, the tenancy can be renewed for a shorter period.

Assured tenancies

At the beginning of an assured tenancy, it will be classed as a 'contractual assured tenancy' for a fixed period. The tenancy automatically becomes a 'statutory assured tenancy' if:

- the landlord ends the tenancy by issuing a notice to quit (eg because they want to change the agreement) and the tenant stays in the property
- the fixed period covered by the tenancy comes to an end and the tenant stays in the property

There are different rights and responsibilities on both landlord and tenant depending on the type of assured tenancy.

Other types of tenancy

Most tenancies in Scotland issued before December 2017 are short assured or assured tenancies. The other tenancy types are:

- 'Common law' tenancy - if a tenant shares their home as a lodger
- regulated tenancy - the most common form of tenancy before 1989
- agricultural tenancy
- crofting tenancy

'Common law' tenancies

If a landlord is sharing their house or flat with their tenants, they can't use the short assured or assured tenancy. Instead, they will automatically have what is known as a 'common law tenancy'. The tenant doesn't have to have a written contract, but the landlord may use a lodger agreement to create a contract between them and the tenant - so both are clear about what has been agreed. (See appendix for sample lodger agreement).

Regulated tenancies

Tenancies created before 2 January 1989 are generally regulated tenancies. As not many exist we will not be describing them further here.

Agricultural tenancies

There are 3 types of agricultural tenancy:

- limited duration tenancy - if the lease is for more than 5 years
- short, limited duration tenancy - if the lease is for 5 years or less
- 1991 Act tenancy - if the tenancy began before 2003

All agricultural tenants have the right to:

- a written lease
- compensation at the end of the tenancy for any improvements they made to the land during their tenancy
- leave the tenancy to a spouse or relative in their will
- If the lease is over 5 years, agricultural tenants can also:
- pass their tenancy on to a relative or spouse within their lifetime
- use the land for non-agricultural purposes
- Tenants with a 1991 Act tenancy have the right to buy the land they are leasing.

If there's a house on the land, both landlord and tenant have obligations to keep it in good repair.

Crofting tenancies

Crofting is a system of landholding unique to the Highlands and Islands of Scotland. Usually, the crofter holds the croft on the 'statutory conditions' and doesn't have a written lease. Crofting is regulated by the Crofting Commission. The tenant must get written agreement from the Commission if you want to make any changes to a crofting tenancy (including a change of tenant).

What the landlord must include in a tenancy agreement
If a landlord used an assured or short assured tenancy, the agreement must be written down. It must include:

- the names of all people involved
- the rental price and how it's paid
- the deposit amount and how it will be protected (see below)
- when the deposit can be fully or partly withheld (eg to repair damage caused by tenants)
- the property address
- the start and end date of the tenancy
- any tenant or landlord obligations
- who's responsible for minor repairs
- which bills your tenants are responsible for
- a statement telling the tenant that antisocial behaviour is a breach of the agreement

For other types of tenancy, it's still good practice to put the agreement in writing, including other information. To avoid any confusion later, the landlord can include other information in the agreement, such as:

- whether the tenancy can be ended early and how this can be done
- information on how and when the rent will be reviewed
- whether the property can be let to someone else (sublet) or have lodgers

Changes to tenancy agreements
The landlord must get the agreement of their tenants if they want to make changes to the terms of their tenancy agreement.

Preventing discrimination

Unless the landlord has a very strong reason, they must change anything in a tenancy agreement that might discriminate against tenants on the grounds of:

- gender
- sexual orientation
- disability (or because of something connected with their disability)
- religion or belief
- being a transsexual person
- the tenant being pregnant or having a baby

Ending a Short-assured tenancy

To get a property back, the landlord must give tenants a 'notice to quit' and a 'Section 33 notice'. For a short-assured tenancy, the minimum notice period is 40 days if the tenancy is for 6 months or longer.

For a tenancy that is continuing on a month-by-month basis after the original period has ended, the notice period is a minimum of 28 days. The landlord must give 2 months notice when giving a Section 33 notice. They can issue both the notice to quit and Section 33 notice at the same time. (See appendix)

Other tenancy types (excluding the new private residential tenancy)

For other tenancy types the landlord must give at least:

- 28 days if the tenancy is for up to 1 month
- 31 days if the tenancy is for up to 3 months
- 40 days if the tenancy is for more than 3 months

Ending a tenancy early
A landlord can end a tenancy early if:
- the tenant breaks a condition of the tenancy agreement
- landlord and tenant agree to end the tenancy

If tenants don't leave
If the notice period expires and tenants don't leave the property, the landlord can start the process of eviction through the courts. A landlord must tell tenants of their intention to get a court order by giving them a 'notice of intention to raise proceedings' (AT6) (see appendix).

If tenants want to leave
The tenancy agreement should say how much notice tenants need to give before they can leave the property. If the notice isn't mentioned in the tenancy agreement, the minimum notice a tenant can give is:
- 28 days if their tenancy runs on a month-to-month basis (or if it's for less than a month)
- 40 days if their tenancy is for longer than 3 months

Unless there's a break clause in the tenancy agreement, a landlord can insist that their tenants pay rent until the end of the tenancy. If tenants leave the property without giving notice, or before the notice has run out, they're still responsible for the property and the rent by law.

Houses in multiple occupation (HMOs)
If a tenant is living in a bedsit, shared flat, lodging, shared house, hostel or bed and breakfast accommodation it's likely that they will be living a house in multiple occupation or 'HMO'. A landlord will have an HMO if:

- tenants live with two or more other people, and
- they don't belong to the same family, and
- they share some facilities, e.g., a bathroom or kitchen, and
- the accommodation is their only or main home (if they are a student, their term-time residence counts as their main home).

If they live with a homeowner their family doesnt count as 'qualifying persons' when deciding whether a property is an HMO. So, for example, if they share accommodation with the owner and one other unrelated lodger, they won't live in an HMO. If they live with the owner and two other unrelated lodgers, they will live in an HMO. Before the council gives a landlord an HMO licence, it will carry out the following checks:

Is the landlord a fit and proper person to hold a licence?
Before it will grant an HMO licence, the council must check that the owner and anyone who manages the property (for example, a letting agent) don't have any criminal convictions, for example, for fraud or theft.

Is the property managed properly?
The council must check that the landlord respects tenants' legal rights. They should be given a written tenancy agreement stating clearly what the landlord's responsibilities are, and what the tenants responsibilities are. This should cover things like rent, repairs, and other rules. To manage the property properly, the landlord must:
- keep the property and any furniture and fittings in good repair
- deal with the tenant fairly and legally when it comes to rent and other payments, for example they:

- must go through the correct procedure if they want to increase the rent
- cannot resell the tenant gas or electricity at a profit
- not evict the tenant illegally
- make sure that their tenants don't annoy or upset other people living in the area.

Does the property meet the required standards?
To meet the standards expected of an HMO property:

- the rooms must be a decent size, for example, every bedroom should be able to accommodate a bed, a wardrobe, and a chest of drawers.
- there must be enough kitchen and bathroom facilities for the number of people living in the property, with adequate hot and cold-water supplies.
- adequate fire safety measures must be installed, for example the landlord must provide smoke alarms and self-closing fire doors and make sure there is an emergency escape route.
- all gas and electrical appliances must be safe.
- heating, lighting, and ventilation must all be adequate.
- the property should be secure, with good locks on the doors and windows.
- there must be a phone line installed so that tenants can set up a contract with a phone company to supply the service.

What are the landlord's responsibilities?
To keep their HMO licence, a landlord must maintain the property properly:

- **Common parts** - these must be kept clean and in good repair (for example, the stairwell, hall, shared kitchen, and bathroom). However, the landlord can include a clause in the tenancy agreement which passes this responsibility onto the tenants.

- **Shared facilities** - these should be kept in good repair (for example, the cooker, boiler, fridge, sinks, bath, and lighting)
- **Heating, hot water and ventilation** - these facilities must all be kept in good order
- **Gas safety** - all gas appliances and installations must be safe (for example, a gas fire, boiler or cooker) - these should be checked once a year by a Gas Safe Register engineer
- **Electrical safety** - all electrical appliances and installations must be safe - these should be tested every three years by a contractor approved by the National Inspection Council for Electrical Installation Contracting (NICEIC) or SELECT, Scotland's trade association for the electrical, electronics and communications systems industry
- **Fire precautions** - all fire precautions (for example, smoke alarms and fire extinguishers) must be in good working order and that the fire escape route is kept safe and free from obstructions
- **Furniture** - all furniture supplied must meet safety standards (for example, isn't flammable)
- **Roof, windows, and exterior** - these must all be adequately maintained
- **Rubbish** - enough rubbish bins must be provided
- **Deposits** - tenants deposits must be returned within a reasonable time when they move out, preferably within 14 days.

The landlord should also put-up notices in the accommodation:

- giving the name and address of the person responsible for managing it so that the tenant can contact them whenever necessary
- explaining what the tenant should do in an emergency, for example if there is a gas leak or a fire.

Tenants' responsibilities:

- **Repairs** – the tenant should let the landlord know if anything in the property needs repairing, particularly if this is something they are responsible for keeping in good order, such as the roof, boiler, or toilet
- **Damage** – the tenant must take good care of the property and try not to damage anything
- **Rubbish** - not let rubbish pile up in or around the property but dispose of it properly in the bins provided
- **Inspections** - let the landlord inspect the property so they can check whether any maintenance work needs doing. Normally this should happen once every six months. The landlord must give you 24 hours' written notice before coming round.
- **Behave responsibly** - make sure that the tenant doesnt behave in a way that can annoy or upset neighbours. The landlord is responsible for dealing with any complaints made by neighbours and must act if they are unhappy with tenants' behaviour.

Safeguarding Tenancy Deposits

A tenancy deposit scheme is a scheme provided by an independent third party to protect deposits until they are due to be repaid. Three schemes are now operating:

- Letting Protection Service Scotland
- Safedeposits Scotland
- Mydeposits Scotland

Landlord's legal duties

The legal duties on landlords who receive a tenancy deposit are:
- to pay deposits to an approved tenancy deposit scheme
- to provide the tenant with key information about the tenancy and deposit

Key dates for landlords

The dates by which landlords must pay deposits to an approved scheme and provide information to the tenant vary, depending on when the deposit was received:

1. Deposit received prior to 7 March 2011:

Where the tenancy is renewed by express agreement or tacit relocation on or after 2 October 2012 and before 2 April 2013 (Regulation 47(a))

Within 30 working days of renewal. In any other case by 15 May 2013

2. Deposit received on or after 7 March 2011 and before 2 July 2012

By 13 November 2012

3. Deposit received on or after 2 July 2012 and before 2 October 2012

By 13 November 2012

4. Deposit received on or after 2 October 2012

Within 30 working days of the beginning of the tenancy

Information about the schemes

Further details about the individual schemes are available on the individual scheme web sites below. Email addresses and telephone numbers are also included. All three schemes have a range of information available for landlords (and their agents) as well as tenants and these include how landlords can join the schemes, how to submit deposits, how to ask for repayment of deposits and how the dispute resolution service will work.

Letting Protection Service Scotland

www.lettingprotectionscotland.com
Address:
The Pavilions
Bridgwater Road
Bristol
BS99 6BN
Email contact: events@lettingprotectionscotland.com
Telephone: 0330 303 0031

SafeDeposits Scotland

www.safedepositsscotland.com
Address:
Lower Ground
250 West George Street
Glasgow
G2 4QY
Email contact: info@safedepositsscotland.com
Telephone: 03333 213 136

Mydeposits Scotland

www.mydepositsscotland.co.uk
Address:
Premiere House

Elstree Way Borehamwood
Hertfordshire
WD6 1JH
Email contact: info@mydepositsscotland.co.uk
Telephone: 0333 321 9402

****

Ch.10

RELATIONSHIP BREAKDOWN-RIGHTS OF OCCUPATION IN THE HOME

Rights in the home

The main areas of law covering rights to remain in the home are The Family Law Act 1996, The Matrimonial Causes Act 1973, the Civil Partnerships Act 2004, and the Marriage (Same Sex Couples) Act 2013. There are other areas of law covering domestic violence, i.e. The Domestic Violence, Crime and Victims Act 2004. In 2015, new legislation was introduced which criminalised the use of 'controlling or coercive behaviour in an intimate or family relationship' through the Serious Crime Act 2015 (section 76), which was introduced to prevent emotional or psychological abuse in domestic scenarios. Further Acts are in the pipeline. In Scotland there is the Domestic Abuse Act 2018. In Northern Ireland, The Family Homes, and Domestic Violence (Northern Ireland) Order 1998. Further law is being prepared in Northern Ireland, as in England and Wales.

Whatever the circumstances, a person has the right to remain in the family home following a spilt from a partner if a person has legal ownership of the property (i.e., the sole or joint owner, or sole or joint tenant. These are known as "pre-existing housing rights" and are not dependent on a person's relationship or whether they have dependent children. These rights give a person:

- The right to remain in the property unless excluded by a court order
- Occupation of the accommodation by the sole tenant or any of the joint tenants will maintain secure, assured, or assured shorthold tenancies
- The right to pay the mortgage/rent (they will also be liable for any arrears)
- The right to exclude others from the property. A joint tenant will not be able to exclude another joint tenant without a court order
- An automatic right to defend possession proceedings
- The right to end a tenancy. For periodic tenancies one joint tenant acting alone could end the tenancy for all joint tenants
- If owned, the owner has the right to sell the property, but all joint owners will need to agree to the sale

A person can also have pre-existing housing rights if they have a beneficial interest in the property even if they do not have legal ownership of the property. Non owners can attain beneficial interest if:

- The non owner paid money directly towards the acquisition of a property unless it was clearly made as a gift, the non owner may be able to claim a beneficial interest in the property
- The non owner only made indirect financial contributions such as paying the bills, they can only claim beneficial interest if there is some understanding that the non owner is to get a share of the property. There must be evidence of this understanding, but it does not have to be in writing. This is known as constructive trust.

If the non owner has made no financial contributions but has acted to their detriment (such as selling another home or giving up some of worth like a secure tenancy), in reliance of a promise that they would obtain a share if the property then this may give rights similar to beneficial interest by the way of common law proprietary estoppel. Such cases are rare.

Note that unless the non owner has made some sort of financial contribution to the purchase or improvement of the property, and there is documented evidence of the intention to give beneficial interest it is very difficult to establish that a non owner has beneficial interest in a property.

If a person has beneficial interest in a property, they will have the right to:

- Occupy the property (in most cases)
- A share of the proceeds once the property is sold
- Force or delay a sale of the property, but they will need to obtain a court order to do this

The non owning partner or the former partner will need to apply for an order under s14 Trusts of Land and Appointment of Trustees Act 1996 (TLATA) for a "declaration of interests".

Who does not have pre-existing rights?
A person will not have any housing rights if:
- The tenancy is solely in the name of the partner
- The property is owned by the partner
- They will only have the right to occupy the property for as long as the partner gives them "permission" to live there.

Under housing law:

- They are usually only entitled to reasonable notice to leave from their partner
- The landlord/mortgage company can refuse to accept payments of rent/mortgage from them, even if the partner is not paying. They will however have the right to claim housing benefit
- If the partner is an assured or secure tenant who has left the property permanently it may be harder for the client to stay in the property
- Even if the sole tenant/owner does leave the landlord/lender must still apply for an order from the county court if they wish to evict them
- They can not defend possession proceedings from the landlord or lender

Home rights for spouse / civil partner of tenants.
A non tenant spouse/civil partner have the rights to:

- Occupy the property even if asked to leave by their tenant spouse/civil partner Occupy the property even after their tenant spouse/civil partner has left and will maintain a secure or assured tenancy
- Pay rent to the landlord
- Defend possession proceedings
- The non tenant spouse/civil partner will not be liable for rent arrears of his/her partner (although the landlord may terminate the partner's tenancy based on those arrears, so the non tenant may have to pay towards the arrears as well as the current rent to preserve the tenancy)

- The non tenant spouse/civil partner may, however, be liable for court costs and mesne profits for refusing to leave after a possession order has expired

To protect their home rights against third parties the non tenant spouse/civil partner should notify the landlord of their presence and the marriage/civil partnership.

Home rights for spouse/civil partner of owners.

A non tenant spouse/civil partner has the right to:

- Occupy the property even if asked to leave by their tenant spouse/civil partner
- Pay the mortgage
- Defend possession proceedings
- The non tenant spouse/civil partner will not be liable for mortgage arrears of his/her partner (but the non tenant may have to pay towards the arrears as well as the current instalments to prevent repossession by the lender)
- The non owner spouse/civil partner may, however, be liable for court costs for refusing to leave if the mortgage lender applies for a warrant of possession after a possession order has expired. The mortgage lender has no obligation to inform the spouse/civil partner of the borrower about any arrears, the onus is therefore on the spouse/civil partner to make enquires and find out what the situation is.

To protect home rights against third parties the non tenant spouse/civil partner should inform the mortgage company of their marriage.

If there is a threat that the owning spouse may sell the property, then the non owning spouse/civil partner can complete form HR1 and

113

apply to the Land Registry to put a notice on the land register. This notice does not mean that the property cannot be sold but if anyone brought the property with the notice in place, then they would be bound by any future decision the court makes about disposal of the property. Subsequently, no buyer would go ahead with the purchase when such a notice is in place. Please note that the owning spouse/civil partner will be informed when the notice is made.

Home rights for Cohabitees, ex-cohabitees, and divorcees.
Cohabitees, ex-cohabitees, and divorcees do not automatically have home rights – they will first have to apply to court of an occupation order. An occupation order is an order from the court that may grant temporary home rights and are usually short-term measures to allow the parties' time to pursue more long-term housing solutions. The court will be very reluctant to grant occupation orders unless there is current domestic violence or to protect children.

****

Chapter 11

THE LAW AND OWNER OCCUPIERS- COMMONHOLD, FREEHOLD AND LEASEHOLD

Commonhold and Leasehold Reform Act 2002

The Commonhold and Leasehold Reform Act 2002 introduced into English law an entirely new form of tenure, namely commonhold. It is specifically targeted at blocks of flats, where leasehold has been the normal form of tenure until now. We will discuss commonhold briefly a little later, suffice to say that with such an arrangement in a block of flats the commonholders own all the common parts together with leases being abolished. As we discussed earlier, the government has banned the sale of new build leasehold houses and wishes there to be a move towards commonhold as a form of ownership.

Freehold and Leasehold

For practical purposes, the strongest form of title to land is that of freehold. Freehold title lasts forever; it may be bought and sold or passed by inheritance. In short, freehold title is tantamount to outright ownership, and is taken as such for the purposes of this book.

Freeholders may, of course, use their land for their own purposes. The freehold homeowner is merely the most familiar example. But they may also, if they wish, allow other people to use their land. And this is where leases, and other forms of tenure, come in.

A lease grants the leaseholder permission to use the land for a certain period, which can be anything from a day or two to several thousand years. It will usually attach conditions, for example that the leaseholder must pay a ground rent. Recently, in 2018 there has been a growing scandal concerning ground rents, with many developers selling off freeholds to private companies who charge exorbitant ground rents.

The lease may, but does not have to, put certain restrictions on what the leaseholder may do with the land. But it must, to be a lease rather than merely a licence, grant the leaseholder 'exclusive possession'. This is the right to exclude other people, especially the landlord, from the land. Such a right need not be absolute, and exceptions to it are explained later in the book: but it is enough to give the leaseholder a high degree of control over the land, which has become, for the duration of the lease, very much the leaseholder's land rather than the freeholders.

A lease, unless it contains a stipulation to the contrary, may be bought, sold, or inherited; if this happens, all the rights and duties under it pass to the new owner.

Leases and Tenancies

Confusion is often caused by the fact that, although the terms leaseholder (or lessee) and tenant are legally interchangeable, they tend to be used in different senses. The tendency is to refer to short leases as tenancies: the more substantial the rights conferred, and the longer the period for which they run, the likelier it is that the agreement will be referred to as a lease.

Types of Leasehold Property

In the context of residential property, it should be noted that the great majority of leases relate to flats rather than houses. This is because of the legal concept of land tenure as described above. If a builder buys some freehold land and covers it in houses, it is possible to parcel out the area so that each bit of freehold land, and the house standing on it, can be sold separately. It does not matter if the houses are semi-detached or terraced, because there is well-established law governing party walls of adjoining freeholders.

Where flats are sold, each purchaser acquires a lease that gives him specified rights over the parcel of land on which the flats stand. These rights, of course, are shared by the leaseholders of the other flats. In addition, however, each leaseholder gains the right to exclusive possession of part of the building occupying the land - his own flat. The leaseholder would say "I own my flat", but the law says, "He owns a lease granting him certain rights, that of access, to a defined parcel of land and the right of exclusive possession of specified parts of a building erected on that land." This may seem a slightly unusual way of looking at it, but it is fundamental to understanding the way that the law sees the relationship between leaseholders of flats and their freeholders.

The freehold of flatted property will often be retained by the developer, although sometimes it will be sold to a property company. Formerly, it was common practice for the freehold to be retained even when separate houses were built. This allowed the freeholder to retain an interest in the property and, above all, to regain full possession of it when the lease expired. However, the position of freeholders has been weakened by three key pieces of legislation, the Leasehold Reform Act 1967, the Leasehold Reform, Housing and Urban Development Act 1993, and the Commonhold and Leasehold Reform Act 2002. These Acts are described in detail further on, their overall effect is to entitle leaseholders either to the freehold of houses or to a new lease of flats. In view of the legislation, there is now little point in the original owner's attempting to retain the freehold of land on which houses have been built. The exception is where a house is sold based on shared ownership - see below.

Most residential leasehold property therefore consists of flats. Of these, most are in the private sector, comprising purpose-built blocks and (especially in London) conversions of what were once large single houses. The freehold will usually belong to the developer, to a property company, or sometimes to the original owner of the site.

In flats, although the leaseholder will normally be responsible for the interior of the flat, the freeholder will maintain the fabric of the building and will recoup the costs of doing so by levying service charges on the leaseholders. This is an area of such potential conflict between leaseholders and freeholders that it has been the subject of legislation. It is dealt with fully further on in the book.

Ground rents
The freeholder will charge leaseholders a ground rent. However, there has been much controversy concerning ground rents with developers imposing unreasonable sums which escalate and make flats un-saleable. Following numerous court cases and government intervention, leaseholders trapped by this unscrupulous practice and now receiving compensation and redress.

Mixed-tenure blocks: the right to buy
Sometimes flats have been sold in blocks that were originally developed for letting to tenants: the result is often a 'mixed-tenure' block, with both leaseholders and tenants. Although this sometimes happens in the private sector, it is particularly common in blocks owned by local authorities and housing associations, for it is to these that the statutory right to buy applies. This right was created by the Housing Act 1980 and allows most local authority tenants, and some

118

housing association tenants, to buy their homes at a heavily discounted price. Tenants of houses are normally sold the freehold, but tenants of flats become leaseholders.

Shared ownership

Another result of the trend towards home ownership has been the dramatic expansion of shared ownership. This is a form of tenure that combines leasing and renting. However, the term 'shared ownership' is something of a misnomer because ownership is not, in fact, shared between the leaseholder and the freeholder. The leaseholder pays less than the full value of the lease; typically, half. In exchange for this concession, he pays not the normal notional ground rent but a much more substantial rent. However, he is much more a leaseholder than he is a tenant, and, like other leaseholders (but unlike tenants) is responsible for the internal repair of the property and, in the case of houses, usually the fabric of the building too.

Shared owners usually have the right to increase their stake as and when they can afford it: this is called 'staircasing' because the owner's share goes up in steps. If the property is a house, the freehold will normally be transferred when the owner's share reaches 100%, and he will then be in the same position as any other freehold homeowner. If it is a flat, he will continue to be a leaseholder but there will no longer be a rental (other than ground rent).

Commonhold

To try to deal with problems arising from the relationship between freeholders and leaseholders, a new form of tenure, 'commonhold', was created by the Commonhold and Leasehold Reform Act 2002. It is designed specifically for use in blocks of flats, and the idea is that all the individual flat owners (or 'unit holders', as the Act calls them) will

119

belong to a 'commonhold association', a registered company that operate under a constitution (the 'memorandum and articles') and act in accordance with a 'commonh*old community statement'. This arrangement ensures that each unit holder will have two separate interests in relation to the property: individually, and collectively, in the block.

As mentioned in the introduction the government is in favour of moving away from leasehold property to commonhold and, for a start, has banned the sale of all new build leasehold houses.

****

Chapter 12

OBLIGATIONS OF FREEHOLDER AND LEASEHOLDER

General Principles

For centuries the law did little to regulate the relationship between freeholders and leaseholders.

In the twentieth century, however, the view grew up that some types of bargains are inherently unfair and even those that are not might still be open to exploitation.

An example of the first type is an agreement that residential property will revert to the original freeholder at the end of a long lease. This meant that when 99-year leases expired, leaseholders found that their homes had abruptly returned to the outright ownership of the heir of the original freeholder, leaving them as mere trespassers liable to be ejected at any time. In practice, freeholders were usually willing to grant a fresh lease, but sometimes only at a very high price that the leaseholder might well be unable to afford. In some cases, freeholders insisted on reclaiming the property however much the leaseholder offered, and the law supported them. This is the situation that led to legislation entitling almost all residential leaseholders to extend their leases, and many of them to claim the freehold.

The freeholder's right to demand a service charge is an example of an arrangement that is fair in principle but open to abuse in practice. It is inevitable, especially in flats that responsibility for some types of repairs cannot be ascribed to any individual leaseholder and must therefore be retained by the freeholder, who must, in turn, recoup the cost from leaseholders. However, some freeholders abused this system by levying extravagant service charges that made the service charge a source of profit. To prevent this, there is now a substantial body of legislation designed to ensure that freeholders carry out only the works that are necessary and that they recover their legitimate costs and no more. The complicated rules governing this are chiefly found in the Landlord and Tenant Act 1985 (as amended).

Under the Landlord and Tenant Act 1987,as amended, either party to a long lease (one originally granted for at least 21 years) may go to the First Tier Tribunal to argue that the lease is deficient in some way and needs to be changed. If only the one lease is affected, the tribunal may vary it. Sometimes, however, several leases may need to be changed; in this case either the freeholder or 75% of the leaseholders may apply.

Obligations of Leaseholders

The obligations of leaseholders are set out in the lease; indeed, since it is a document drafted by or on behalf of freeholders, one of its main aims is to tell leaseholders what they must and must not do. However, legislation and judicial decisions sometimes come to the leaseholder's assistance.

Consumer legislation can also apply to leases; in particular, the Unfair Terms in Consumer Contracts Regulations 1999 (which replace earlier regulations made in 1995) have a major impact. Also, the Consumer Rights Act 2015 has a significant bearing. These apply to standard terms in contracts. This means they normally cover the terms of leases, which are usually presented to potential leaseholders as a package with no opportunity to renegotiate individual terms. Occasionally, however, individual terms can be specifically negotiated, and it should be noted that in that case the Unfair Terms Regulations do not apply. Nor will they apply to any lease granted before the earlier version of the regulations which came in July 1995. The now disbanded Office of Fair Trading issued advice about the types of term that are likely to be judged unfair in the context of assured tenancies. The OFT closed on 01 April 2014, with its responsibilities passing to a number of different organisations including the Competition and Markets Authority (CMA) and the Financial Conduct Authority

a: Plain and intelligible language
An increasing number of modern leases are being written in more intelligible language, and for leases made since 1995 the Unfair Terms Regulations mean that arcanely written terms may be unenforceable. However, a huge number of leases written in traditional style still have decades or even centuries to run, so unfortunately property lawyers' English will be with us for a long time yet.

b: Terms Unfair on Consumers
These are terms that place an unreasonable burden on the customer (the leaseholder) or give an unfair advantage to the supplier (the freeholder). Some of these terms are common in long leases.

There may be a clause in which the leaseholder declares that he has 'read and understood' the lease, even though the document is long and complex and it unlikely that anyone would read (or understand) the whole of it. The aim is to put the leaseholder at a disadvantage in any dispute by arguing that he was fully aware of all the terms of the lease. Another way of loading the scales is a clause allowing the freeholder the final decision about vital matters, such as whether the freeholder and the leaseholder have fulfilled their respective obligations under the lease.

These clauses are probably unenforceable in leases made since July 1995, but in earlier leases they are probably valid.

There are other types of clauses that are potentially a problem for the leaseholder. An example is a clause laying down procedural formalities. Such a clause is not necessarily a problem: for instance, leases commonly require formal communications between the freeholder and the leaseholder to be in writing, and this is a perfectly reasonable requirement because it reduces the chances misunderstandings or disputes about who said what. But it is harder to justify a requirement for notices to be sent by registered post, and some leases stipulate procedures that are so onerous that the aim seems to be to deter leaseholders from exercising their rights.

Similar comments apply to clauses imposing financial penalties for breaches of the lease. This is not necessarily unreasonable, but sometimes the penalties are out of all proportion to the nature of the breach.

Some leases require the leaseholder to join with the freeholder (and help with the cost) in responding to legal or other notices pertaining to the property. Again, this may be reasonable in some circumstances, but as a blanket requirement it can act against leaseholders' interests.

The possibility that unfair, or potentially unfair, clauses will feature in a lease underlines the need for competent legal advice before signing it. An experienced solicitor will be able to advise whether doubtful clauses can be, or are likely to be, used against leaseholders. Leaseholders may also have remedies available under the Landlord and Tenant Act: this is covered below and, in the key area of service charges, in the next Chapter.

c: Restrictive clauses in leases
So far, we have looked at leases as if they were consumer contracts and outlined some of the clauses, they may contain that could affect leaseholders in their capacity as consumers. But there are some further potentially difficult terms that relate specifically to property issues. These terms are not necessarily unreasonable. For example, in a lease concerning an upstairs flat it would be quite

normal to have a clause requiring the leaseholder to keep the premises carpeted. This makes sense because bare floors, although currently very fashionable, could be very noisy for the people in the flat below.

It is easy to see why freeholders want such clauses in the lease: it is because they realise that there will be serious problems if someone attempts, for instance, to keep four Alsatians in a studio flat. The neighbours will be inconvenienced and will complain to the freeholder, and leases of other flats in the same block will become difficult to sell. The same arguments could apply if one of the leaseholders allows his flat to fall into complete decorative decay or if he runs a noisy and busy trade from his home.

But the kind of blanket rules that appear in many leases go too far. A rule against any pets at all forbids not only four noisy Alsatians but also entirely inoffensive pets such as a budgie or a goldfish. In the same way, prohibiting business activities means that the leaseholder may not use his home to write a book for publication, or address envelopes, and so on - types of home working that could not possibly inconvenience anyone.

The rule against sub-letting also prevents leaseholders from exploiting the value of their property by letting it out, something that is open to most homeowners and is increasingly accepted as normal.

d: Restrictions on sale

Some leases restrict the kind of person to whom the lease may be sold (or 'assigned' - see below). For example, a housing scheme may have been intended specifically for the elderly. Clearly, it will not be maintained as such if leaseholders are free to assign or bequeath their leases to whomever they please, so the lease will say that it may be assigned only to persons above a certain age, and that if it is inherited by anyone outside the age group it must be sold on to someone qualified to hold it. Although this could be described as an onerous term because it makes it more difficult to find a buyer and may reduce the lease's value, it is reasonable given the need to ensure that the scheme continues to house elderly people exclusively. And the restriction it imposes is not too severe because so many potential purchasers qualify.

However, some leases define much more narrowly to whom they may be sold. Sometimes the freeholder is a body owned and run by the leaseholders themselves, and in these cases, it is usual to require that all leaseholders must join the organisation and, if they leave it, must immediately dispose of the lease to someone that is willing to join. Again, such a term is not necessarily unacceptable. If the organisation makes relatively light demands on its members (perhaps no more than a modest admission fee or annual subscription), the restriction is unlikely greatly to diminish the value of the lease. If, however, the organisation expects much more from its members - perhaps that they actively take part in running it, or that they pay a large annual subscription - the value of the lease will be severely reduced because it will be difficult to find purchasers willing to accept the conditions. A key point is whether the organisation has power to expel members, thus forcing them to sell; and, if so, in what circumstances and by whom this power can be exercised.

e: Access
Virtually any lease will contain a clause allowing the freeholder to enter the property to inspect or repair it. This has the effect of qualifying the leaseholder's right of exclusive possession (see below), but only subject to certain conditions. The freeholder (or the freeholder's servants, such as agents or contractors) may enter only at reasonable times, and subject to the giving of reasonable notice. If these conditions are not met, the leaseholder is under no obligation to allow them in; and, even when the conditions are met, the landlord will be trespassing if he enters the property without

the leaseholder's consent. If the leaseholder refuses consent even though the time is reasonable and reasonable notice has been given, the landlord's remedy is to get a court order against the leaseholder compelling him to grant entry. It is probable, in such a case, that the landlord will seek, and get, an award of legal costs against the leaseholder.

f: Arbitration
Many leases contain clauses providing those disputes can be submitted to arbitration at the request of either party. By the Commonhold and Leasehold Reform Act, the effect of these clauses is limited, because the results will not be binding so far as the First Tier Tribunal is concerned. If, however, once a dispute has arisen, the parties to agree to submit it to an agreed arbitrator, they are bound by the result, which is enforceable by the courts. If such a 'post-dispute' arbitration finds that the leaseholder is in breach, this is equivalent to a finding by the First Tier Tribunal and will (if the other requirements are met) allow the freeholder to proceed with forfeiture. Arbitration may be a useful mechanism in some cases, and it may be cheaper and quicker than legal action, but it may be difficult to find an arbitrator in whom both parties have confidence.

Obligations of Freeholders
a: Exclusive possession and quiet enjoyment
The first and most important obligation on the freeholder, without which there would be no legal lease at all, is to respect the leaseholder's rights of 'exclusive possession' and 'quiet enjoyment'. Exclusive possession is the right to occupy the property and exclude others from it, especially the freeholder. Quiet enjoyment is another way of underlining the leaseholder's rights over the property: it means that the freeholder may not interfere with the leaseholder's use of the property provided that the terms of the

lease are observed.

However, the leaseholder's right to quiet enjoyment applies only to breaches by the freeholder or the freeholder's servants such as agents or contractors. It is important to note this because the term is sometimes thought to mean that the freeholder must protect the leaseholder against any activity by anyone that interferes with his use of the property: this is not so. For example, if the freeholder carries out some activity elsewhere in the building that interferes with the leaseholder, the leaseholder's right to quiet enjoyment has been breached and he is entitled to redress unless the freeholder can show that the activity was necessary, for instance to comply with repairing obligations under the lease. But if the interference is caused by someone else, perhaps another leaseholder, the freeholder's obligation to provide quiet enjoyment has not been breached. And it is worth stressing in this connection that even if the other leaseholder is in breach of his lease, it is entirely up to the freeholder whether to act. Other leaseholders have no power to force the freeholder to deal with the situation.

This means that if one leaseholder is breaking his lease by holding noisy parties late at night, the other leaseholders may ask, but may not require, the freeholder to take action to enforce the lease. They may, however, take legal action directly against the offending leaseholder for nuisance.

b: The 'section 48' notice

Another important protection for leaseholders is found in section 48 of the Landlord and Tenant Act 1987. This was designed to deal with the situation in which freeholders seek to avoid their responsibilities by (to put it bluntly) doing a disappearing act. Sometimes freeholders would provide no address or telephone number or other means of contact, meaning that leaseholders were unable to hold the freeholder to his side of the agreement. Sections 47 and 48 therefore lay down that the freeholder must formally notify the leaseholder of his name and give an address within England and Wales at which he can be contacted, and that this information must be repeated on every demand for rent or service charge. This has proved especially valuable for leaseholders where the freeholder lives abroad, or is a company based abroad. It should be noted that the address does not have to be the freeholder's home, nor, if the freeholder is a company, its registered office; often it will be the address of a solicitor or property management company, or simply an accommodation address. But the key point is that any notice, or legal writ, is validly served if sent to that address, and the freeholder is not allowed to claim that it never came to his notice.

It is not necessary for the notice required by section 48 to be given in a separate document; it is enough if the name and address is clearly given as part of some other document such as a service charge demand. But if the necessary notice is not given, no payment of rent, service charge, or anything else is due to the freeholder; the leaseholder may lawfully withhold it until section 48 is complied with. But leaseholders withholding payments on this ground must be careful; once the notice is given, it has retrospective effect, so that all the money due to the freeholder then becomes due immediately. Any leaseholder withholding money on the grounds that section 48 has not been complied with should, therefore, make sure that he has the money easily available so that he can pay up if he must.

c: Good management
The freeholder is under an obligation to ensure that his management responsibilities are carried out in a proper and appropriate way. Leaseholders can challenge the freeholder in court or at the FTT if they believe they can show that they are not receiving the standard of management to which they are entitled. This may be an expensive and lengthy process but it better than the

alternative, sometimes resorted to by leaseholders, of withholding rent or service charge. This is risky because, whatever the shortcomings of the freeholder's management, it puts the leaseholders in breach of the conditions of their lease and, as such, demonstrably in the wrong (even if the freeholder may be in the wrong as well).

Withholding due payments is therefore not recommended unless the freeholder is so clearly at fault that arguably no payment is due - for instance, if the service being charged for has clearly not been provided at all (as opposed to being provided inadequately), or if there has been no 'section 48' notice (see above). If leaseholders choose to withhold payment, they are strongly advised to keep the money readily to hand so that they can pay up at once if the freeholder rectifies the problem; the danger otherwise is that they will be taken to court and required to pay immediately to avoid forfeiture (see below).

Powers of Leaseholders over Management
If leaseholders want a scrutiny of the standards of management of their flats, they have power under the Leasehold Reform, Housing and Urban Development Act 1993 to demand a management audit by an auditor acting on behalf of at least two-thirds of the qualifying leaseholders. Qualifying leaseholders are those with leases of residential property originally granted for 21 years or more and requiring them to contribute to the cost of services.

The purpose of the audit, the costs of which must be met by the leaseholders demanding it, is to discover whether the freeholder's duties are being carried out efficiently and effectively. The auditor is appointed by the leaseholders and must be either a qualified accountant or a qualified surveyor and must not live in the block concerned. The auditor has the right to demand papers from the freeholder and can go to court if they are not produced.

Leaseholders' Right to Manage

Leaseholders with long leases (those originally granted for 21 years or more) also have the right to take over management of their block if they wish. This applies to blocks of two or more flats (five or more if there is a resident landlord) and no substantial non-residential part. It does not apply if the freeholder is a local authority.

The leaseholders must first form a 'Right to Manage' company ('RtM' company), which is a limited company whose membership is confined to leaseholders and the freeholder. Before seeking to take over management the RtM company must advise all leaseholders of its intention and invite them to participate. Fourteen days after this invitation and provided the RtM company includes at least half the eligible tenants (or both, if only two are eligible), it can serve a claim notice on the landlord (or on the First Tier Tribunal if the landlord is untraceable) giving at least four months' notice of its intention to take over the management. The landlord has a month to serve a counter-notice objecting to the claim, in which case the LVT will adjudicate. If no counter-notice is served, or if the LVT so decides, the RtM company duly takes over management.

The landlord must end as quickly as possible any existing management arrangements applying to the block. The RtM company takes over the landlord's management functions, including services, repairs, maintenance, improvements, and insurance. The landlord retains its role in respect of any flats without long leaseholders (for example, those let on assured tenancies), and continues to deal with forfeiture (for more on forfeiture see the section below 'If the lease is breached'). Essentially the RtM company steps into the landlord's shoes so far as management is concerned, and it is responsible to both the landlord and the individual leaseholders for the proper carrying out of its functions.

Many leases require the landlord's approval before certain

things can be done, such as assigning the lease or sub-letting. The RtM company takes over this function from the landlord but must consult the landlord before granting approval. If the landlord objects, the matter is referred to the LVT. It seems, however, that refusal of consent by the RtM is final and cannot be challenged by the landlord (although it might be challenged by the leaseholder in question on the ground that the relevant term of the lease is unenforceable). The RtM company has authority to enforce covenants in the lease, but not by means of forfeiture.

At first blush the power to take over management in this way may appear attractive. However, leaseholders should think very carefully before they commit themselves; there are some potential snags.

The biggest problem is one of enforcement. So long as all leaseholders are agreed about what needs to be done and are all willing and able to meet their obligations (including that of paying for services), enforcement will not be an issue, and all will be well. But if some individual leaseholders refuse to pay their share or fail to abide by the covenants in their leases, the RtM company will have to act to enforce the leases, and this may well be difficult. In the first place, any steps to enforce leases will pit neighbour against neighbour and are virtually certain to cause animosity in the block. Secondly, the powerful tool of forfeiture, or threatened forfeiture, is denied to a RtM company. Finally, the RtM company, unlike most freeholders, will not have any substantial financial resources that would allow it to pursue lengthy legal action against individual leaseholders.

There are other issues. The RtM company will depend on the voluntary efforts of its members, and experience shows that many people are not willing to put in the time and effort involved in attending meetings and carrying out essential administration. RtM companies must operate under a special constitution laid down by the Government; the aim of this is to guarantee all leaseholders' rights to be involved, but because the constitution is a standard document applying to all cases it is likely that many leaseholders will find it clumsy and inflexible. Finally, there is the question of continuing relations with the freeholder, which will expect its interests as ultimate owner to be respected by the RtM company.

In short, leaseholders contemplating the formation of a RtM company need to be sure that they are committed not only for the immediate effort of setting it up but for the long haul of carrying out management in the future. They should also recognise that, no matter how united everyone may be to start with, sooner or later the issue of enforcement will rear its head. They should certainly get legal advice about their new responsibilities before committing themselves.

The law allows another remedy in extreme cases of mismanagement. A leaseholder can use the Landlord and Tenant Act 1987, as amended by the Commonhold and Leasehold Reform Act 2002, to force the appointment of a managing agent to run the block instead of the freeholder.

The leaseholder must serve a notice telling the freeholder what the problems are and warning that unless they are put right a First Tier Tribunal will be asked to appoint a managing agent. The FTT may make such an order if it satisfied that it is 'just and convenient'; the Act mentions, as specific examples where this may apply, cases where the freeholder is in breach of obligations under the lease and cases where service charges are being levied in respect of work of a poor standard or an unnecessarily high standard. Note that the procedure is not available if the freeholder is a local authority, a registered housing association, or the Crown.

Recognised Tenants' Association

A recognised tenants' association (RTA), where there is one, has additional rights to be consulted about managing agents. The RTA can serve a notice requiring the freeholder to supply details of the managing agent and the terms of the management agreement.

133

Leaseholders that are receiving a consistently poor or overpriced service may also wish to consider getting rid of the freeholder altogether by collective enfranchisement under the Leasehold Reform, Housing and Urban Development Act 1993 as amended by the CLRA 2002.

Assignment of Leases

One of the most important characteristics of a lease - in marked contrast to most tenancies - is that it may be bought and sold. Usually, the freeholder has no say in this: the leaseholder may sell to whom he likes for the best price he can get, provided that the purchaser agrees to be bound by the terms of the lease. It is, however, usual for the lease to lay down that the freeholder must be informed of any change of leaseholder.

What happens when a lease is sold is that the vendor agrees to transfer to the buyer his rights and obligations under the lease. This is called 'assignment' of the lease. In some types of housing the freeholder has the right to intervene if an assignment is envisaged. The housing may, for instance, be reserved for a particular category of resident, such as the retired, so the freeholder is allowed to refuse consent to the assignment if the purchaser does not qualify.

It was mentioned above that the assignee takes over all the rights and responsibilities attaching to the lease. This means, for instance, that he takes responsibility for any arrears of service charge. Therefore, purchasers' solicitors go to such lengths to ensure that no arrears or other unusual obligations are outstanding.

If the Lease Is Breached

If the terms of a lease are broken, the party offended against can go to court. This may be the leaseholder, for instance if the freeholder has failed to carry out a repair. But it is normally the freeholder that takes the leaseholder to court, for failure to pay ground rent or service charges or for breach of some other requirement.

It is for the court, if satisfied that the lease has been breached, to decide what to do. The normal remedy will be that the offending party must pay compensation and that the breach (if it is continuing) must be put right. It is also likely that the loser will be obliged to pay the winner's legal costs as well as his own, a penalty often considerably more severe that the requirement to pay compensation.

A much more severe remedy open to the freeholder if the leaseholder is in breach is forfeiture of the lease. This means what it says: the lease is forfeit to the freeholder. Forfeiture is sometimes threatened by the more aggressive class of freeholder but the good news for leaseholders is that in practice courts have shown themselves loath to grant it except in very serious cases. Since the Housing Act 1996 took effect, forfeiture for unpaid service charges has been made more difficult for freeholders; this is covered in the next Chapter.

Where forfeiture is threatened for any reason other than failure to pay rent (which, depending on the terms of the lease, may or may not include the service charge element), the freeholder must first serve a 'section 146 notice', so called after the relevant provision of the Law of Property Act 1925. In this he must state the nature of the breach of the lease, what action is required to put it right; if he wants monetary compensation for the breach, the notice must state this too.

Before the section 146 notice can be issued, it must be established that a breach of the lease has occurred. If the leaseholder has admitted the breach, the notice can be issued; otherwise, it must have been decided by a court, the FTT, or an independent arbitrator that the leaseholder is in breach. Moreover, the breach of the lease specified in the section 146 notice must have occurred during the twelve years preceding the notice. For breaches older than this, no valid section 146 notice can be served and so forfeiture is not available. If the notice is not complied with, the freeholder may proceed to forfeit; but the leaseholder may go to court for relief from forfeiture. In practice, courts have generally been willing to grant relief, but they cannot do so unless it is formally applied for. If the leaseholder, perhaps failing to realise the seriousness of the situation, fails to go to court and seek relief, the forfeiture will go ahead. If the freeholder breaches the lease, the leaseholder can go to court and seek an order requiring the freeholder to remedy the breach, to pay damages, or to do both. The commonest type of breach complained of by leaseholders is failure to carry out repairs, and this explains why action by leaseholders is less usual; they know that if they force the freeholder to do repairs the costs will be recovered through service charges. Legal action may be the best course if the dispute affects a single leaseholder; but if several leaseholders are involved, they may well prefer to get rid of the freeholder altogether by collectively enfranchising their leases.

****

Chapter 13

SERVICE CHARGES AND THE LAW

By far the commonest cause of dispute between leaseholders and freeholders is the provision of services and the levying of service charges. In extreme cases, leaseholders have been asked to contribute thousands of pounds towards the cost of major repairs and have even suffered forfeiture of the lease if they are unable, or unwilling, to comply. The Grenfell fie tragedy and the charging to landlords for recladding blocks has been a real issue for leaseholders recently and court battles are still being incurred. As mentioned in the introduction, the government has now put pressure on developers to meet the costs of recladding, and any other associated costs, such as nightwatch. This ensures that leaseholders do not have to bear massive costs, making their flats unsaleable.

The landlord of rented property is expected to meet virtually all costs from the rent, whereas the freeholder of leasehold stock has no rent to fall back on (apart from the normally negligible ground rent). How, then, are major costs to be met when they arise? The answer, of course, is from the service charge, which is, therefore, of central importance to the management of leasehold property.

What goes into a Service Charge?
The lease will say how often service charges are levied: typically, monthly, six-monthly, or annually. It is usual to collect the ground rent at the same time, but this is usually a small component of the bill. The service charge proper will normally consist of three elements.

- **The management fee** is the charge made by the freeholder, or the freeholder's agent, to cover the administrative cost of providing the service and collecting the charge. Usually, it will be much the same amount from one year to the next, but if major works have occurred the management fee will usually be higher to cover the extra costs of appointing and supervising contractors; 15% of the cost of the works is a common figure.

- **Direct costs (routine expenditure)** cover costs such as the supply of electricity to communal areas, building insurance, and the like. Again, these costs are likely to be constant from year to year, so leaseholders   know in advance roughly how much they are likely to   have to pay.

- **Direct costs (exceptional expenditure)** cover costs that are likely to be irregular but heavy. They usually result from maintenance and repair, and it is because this component of the service charge is so unpredictable that it gives rise to so many problems. Where a house has been divided into leasehold flats, the freeholder's costs will usually be like what a normal homeowner would be obliged to pay; in other words, the costs may well be in the thousands (for a new roof, say) but are unlikely to be higher. Even so, a charge of £5000 for a new roof, even if divided between three or four flats, is still a major cost from the point of view of the individual leaseholder, especially if it is unexpected. The situation can be far worse in blocks of flats, where the costs of essential repair and maintenance may run into millions. Replacement of worn-out lifts, for example, is notoriously costly; and costs arising from structural defects are likely to be higher still.

Unreasonable Service Charges-*General Principles*

Sections 18 to 30 of the Landlord and Tenant Act 1985, as amended by the Landlord and Tenant Act 1987, and the Commonhold and Leasehold Reform Act 2002, grant substantial protection to leaseholders of residential property. This protection was introduced after complaints of exploitation by unscrupulous leaseholders, who were alleged to be carrying out unnecessary, or even fictitious, repairs at extravagant prices, whilst not providing the information that would have enabled leaseholders to query the bill. The effect of the Acts is to require freeholders to provide leaseholders with full information about service charges and to consult them before expensive works are carried out.

A few leases, namely those granted under the right to buy by local authorities or registered housing associations, have some additional protection under the Housing Act 1985 (see below), but sections 18 to 30 apply to all residential leases where the service charge depends on how much the freeholder spends. They set out the key rules that freeholders must observe to recover the cost, including overheads, of 'services, repairs, maintenance or insurance', as well as the freeholder's costs of management. It should be noted that failure by leaseholders to pay the service charge does not relieve the freeholder of the obligation to provide the services. The freeholder's remedy is to sue the leaseholder for the outstanding charges, or even to seek forfeiture of the lease (see below). Section 19 of the Landlord and Tenant Act 1985, as amended, provides the key protection to leaseholders by laying down that service charges are recoverable only if they are 'reasonably incurred' and if the services or works are of a reasonable standard. This means that the charge:

o   must relate to some form of 'service, repair, maintenance, or insurance' that the freeholder is required to provide under the lease.
o   must be reasonable (that is, the landlord may not recover costs incurred unnecessarily or extravagantly);
o   - may cover overheads and management costs only if these too are reasonable.

In addition, the charge must normally be passed on to the leaseholders within 18 months of being incurred, and in some cases the freeholder must consult leaseholders before spending the money. These points are covered below.

The Housing Act 1996 (amended by the Commonhold and Leasehold Reform Act 2002) gave leaseholders new powers to refer service charges to the Leasehold Valuation Tribunal (LVT). LVT's have been replaced by First Tier Tribunals (introduced in July 2013)

The First-Tier tribunal
Leaseholders can apply to the First-tier Tribunal (Property Chamber) to deal with disputes about service charges, repairs, extending leases or buying the freehold. This Tribunal was called the Leasehold Valuation Tribunal

What disputes the tribunal deals with
If a person owns a leasehold flat or house and can't resolve a dispute with their freeholder, they may be able to apply to a tribunal for a decision. This tribunal can help with disputes over leasehold problems, such as:

• insuring the building
• the amount billed for service charges

140

- the quality of services such as cleaning and maintenance
- extending a lease
- buying the freehold

How to apply to the tribunal

The tribunal that deals with leaseholder disputes is called the First-tier Tribunal (Property Chamber). There are five regional tribunals. Details of a local tribunal can be found from HM Courts & Tribunals Service.

Costs of taking a case to the tribunal

Leaseholders may have to pay a fee to apply to the tribunal. They can apply for an exemption or a reduced fee if they receive certain benefits or have a low income. If the problem affects more than one leaseholder, they can apply together and share the costs. They may have to pay a surveyor, property manager or a solicitor. In limited cases the tribunal can order the freeholder to compensate them.

If leaseholders win the case, the tribunal may be able to order the freeholder to refund their application fee. Some freeholders can include their legal costs in their service charge bill.

The tribunal's decision

The tribunal's decision is binding on leaseholders and the freeholder. Leaseholders might need to take court action to recover any money the freeholder owes them. The Tribunal can decide:

- Disputes about service charges
- The tribunal can consider if a service charge is payable, and if so how much leaseholders must pay.
- Disputes about repairs

The tribunal can change what a lease says about maintenance and repairs if what's said is unclear or doesn't cover the issue in dispute.

Disputes about poor management

The tribunal can appoint a new manager if a leaseholder can prove their building is being badly managed. The freeholder would still own the property but would lose the right to manage it.

Lease extension disputes

The tribunal can set a price for extending a lease or buying the freehold if the leaseholder and the freeholder haven't been able to agree.

Appeals against the tribunal's decision

A leaseholder may be able to appeal against the tribunal's decision. They can usually only do this if the tribunal has acted unfairly or didn't follow the correct procedures. Leaseholders can't appeal because they don't like the tribunal's decision.

Service Charge demands

Section 153 of the 2002 Commonhold and Leasehold Reform Act states that all demands for service charges must be accompanied by a summary of leaseholder's rights and obligations. Accordingly, a leaseholder can withhold payment of charges if such a summary is not contained with a demand. Where a tenant withholds charges under section 153, the sections of a lease pertaining to payment of charges will not apply for the period for which the charge is withheld.

Consultation with Leaseholders

Section 20 of the LTA 1985, which is the area of the Act dealing with the landlord's obligation to consult leaseholders over both major expenditures, and long-term agreements for the provision of services, has been substituted by section 151 of the 2002 Commonhold and Leasehold Reform Act.

Major works and long-term agreements

Section 151 provides extra protection where the cost of works is more than £250 per leaseholder. Therefore, if a landlord owns a block of 20 flats and wishes to spend £8,000 on repairs, the limit above which he will have to legally consult is £5,000. Costs above this level are irrecoverable (except, sometimes, when the works are urgent) unless the freeholder has taken steps to inform and consult tenants. If the leaseholders are represented by a recognised tenants' association, i.e. formally constituted and recognised by the landlord as well as leaseholders, they must also receive copies of the consultation notices along with individual leaseholders.

In relation to long-term agreements, these are agreements over 12 months. Such agreements may be those for servicing lifts. They do not include contracts of employment. The consultation limit for long term contracts is now £100 per person per annum. If the amount exceeds this, then consultation must be carried out. The steps in the consultation procedure are as follows:

Landlords statement of why works are necessary. There is a requirement for the landlord to state why he considers the works or the agreement to be necessary. This is defined by a 1-month period within which the landlord must take account of all responses from leaseholders. All letters and responses must be prepared in accordance with the requirements of the Act (2002 CLRA).

Estimates. Following this initial stage, at least two estimates must be obtained, of which at least one must be from someone wholly unconnected with the freeholder (obviously a building firm that the freeholder owns or works for is not 'wholly unconnected'; nor is the freeholder's managing agent).

Notification to leaseholders the freeholder must either display a copy of the estimates somewhere they are likely to be seen by everyone liable to pay the service charge, or (preferably) send copies to everyone liable to pay the service charge.

Consultation The notification must describe the works to be carried out and must seek comments and observations, giving a deadline for replies and an address in the UK to which they may be sent. The deadline must be at least a month after the notice was sent or displayed.

Freeholder's response the freeholder must 'have regard' to any representations received. This does not mean, of course, that the freeholder must do what the leaseholders say. It does mean, however, that the freeholder must consider any comments received, and good freeholders often demonstrate that they have done so by sending a reasoned reply.

Therefore, a consultation period will usually be a minimum of 60 days from notification to instructions to carry out works.

If a service charge is challenged in court for failure to follow these procedures, it is a defence for the freeholder to show that the works were urgent. However, the court would need to be satisfied that the urgency was genuine, and that the freeholder behaved reasonably in the circumstances.

Section 151 is important because it gives the leaseholders notification of any unusual items in the offing and gives them an opportunity to raise any concerns and objections. If the leaseholder has any reservations at all, it is vital that they be put before the freeholder at this stage. It is highly unlikely, in the event of legal action later, that the court will support a leaseholder who raised no objection until the bill arrived. It is common for freeholders and their agents to fail to comply with the requirements of section 151. This comment applies not only where the freehold is owned by an individual or a relatively small organisation (where mistakes might be more understandable) but also where the freeholder is a large, well-resourced body like a local authority. As a result, leaseholders are often paying service charges that are not due, so all leaseholders should, before paying a service charge containing unusual items, ensure that section 151, if it applies, has been scrupulously followed. If not, they can refuse to pay.

Service charges held on trust
Section 42 of the Landlord and Tenant Act 1987 (as amended by the 2002 CLRA) further strengthened the position of leaseholders by laying down that the freeholder, or the freeholder's agent, must hold service charge monies in a suitable trust fund that will ensure that the money is protected and cannot be seized by the freeholder's creditors if the freeholder goes bankrupt or into liquidation. However, public sector freeholders, notably local authorities, and registered housing associations, are exempt from this requirement.

Insurance
Usually, the lease provides for the landlord to arrange the insurance of the building (not the contents) and charge the cost as a service charge.

This is the normal arrangement for buildings divided into flats, since it is important that there should be one single policy covering all risks to the building. It is normally recovered as part of the service charges and therefore the cost of the insurance may be challenged before or verified by the LVT in the usual way.

Where a service charge consists of or includes an amount payable for insurance, an individual leaseholder or the secretary of a recognized tenants' association may ask the landlord for a written summary of the policy or an opportunity to inspect and take copies of the policy.

The request must be made in writing and the landlord must comply within 21 days of receiving it.⬚ Where the request is for a written summary, the summary must show:
– the sum for which the property is insured.
– the name of the insurer.
– the risks covered in the policy.
The landlord can only be required to provide the summary once in each insurance period (usually a year).

Where the request is for sight of the policy, the landlord must provide reasonable access for inspection of the policy and any other relevant documents which provide evidence of payment, including receipts, and facilities for copying them. Alternatively, the request may be for the landlord to provide the copies of the policy and specified documents himself and to send them to the leaseholder or association or arrange for them to be collected.

'Period of Grace'
When a dwelling is sold under the right to buy by a local authority or non-charitable housing association, the purchaser is given an estimate of service charges for the following five years. This estimate is the

maximum recoverable during that time. Some purchasers under the right to buy have, however, had a very rude shock when the five-year period of grace expires - see *Exceptionally High Service Charges* below.

The role of a recognised tenants' association

The tenants who are liable to pay for the provision of services may, if they wish, form a recognised tenants' association (RTA) under section 29 of the Landlord and Tenant Act 1985. Note that leaseholders count as tenants for this purpose (see Chapter One, where it explained that legally the two terms are interchangeable). If the freeholder refuses to give a notice recognising the RTA, it may apply for recognition to any member of the local Rent Assessment Committee panel. An important benefit of having a RTA is that it has the right, at the beginning of the consultation process, to recommend persons or organisations that should be invited to submit estimates. However, the freeholder is under no obligation to accept these recommendations.

Another advantage is that the RTA can, whether the freeholder likes it or not, appoint a qualified surveyor to advise on matters relating to service charges. The surveyor has extensive rights to inspect the freeholder's documentation and take copies and can enforce these rights in court if necessary.

Statement of accounts to leaseholders

Under section 152 of the Commonhold and Leasehold Reform Act 2002, which has substituted s.21 of the Landlord and Tenant Act 1985, a landlord must supply a statement of accounts to each tenant by who service charges are payable, in relation to each accounting period. These accounts deal with:

a. Service charges of the tenant and the tenants of dwellings associated with his dwelling

147

b. Relevant costs relating to those service charges
c. The aggregate amount standing to the credit of the tenant and the tenants of those dwellings at the beginning and the end of the accounting period in question.

This statement of account must be supplied to the tenant not later than six months after the accounting period. A certificate of a qualified auditor must be supplied and, in addition, a summary of the rights and obligations of the tenant in relation to service charges must be supplied.

Challenging Service Charges

The Landlord and Tenant Act not only allows leaseholders to act against unreasonable behaviour by the freeholder; it also enables them to take the initiative. This is done in two ways: by giving leaseholders rights to demand information, and by allowing them to challenge the reasonableness of the charge.

Right to require information

Leaseholders have the right to ask freeholders for a written summary of costs counting towards the service charge. This is contained within s.22 of the Landlord and Tenant Act 1985, as amended by s.154 of the Commonhold and Leasehold Reform Act 2002. Such a summary must cover either the twelve months up to the point where it was requested or, if accounts are drawn up annually, the last complete twelve-month accounting period before the request was made. It must be sent to the leaseholder within 21 days of the request or within six months of the end of the period it covers, whichever is the later. Failure to provide it without reasonable excuse is a criminal offence carrying a maximum fine of £2500.

The law lays down some minimum requirements for the summary. It must:

- o cover all the costs incurred during the twelve months it covers, even if they were included in service charge bills of an earlier or later period (see above for late charging and pre-charging);
- o show how the costs incurred by the freeholder are reflected in the service charges paid, or to be paid, by leaseholders.
- o say whether it includes any work covered by a grant (see above);
- o distinguish: (a) those costs incurred for which the freeholder was not billed during the period; (b) those for which he was billed and did not pay; (c) those for which he paid bills.

If it covers five or more dwellings, the summary must, in addition, be certified by a qualified accountant as being a fair summary, complying with the Act, and supported by appropriate documentation. The purpose of section 22, as amended, is to put leaseholders in a position to challenge their service charges. After receiving the summary, the leaseholder has six months in which to ask the freeholder to make facilities available so that he can inspect the documents supporting the summary (bills, receipts, and so on) and take copies or extracts. The freeholder must respond within a month and make the facilities available within the two months following that; the inspection itself must be free, although the freeholder can make a reasonable charge for the copies and extracts. Failure to provide these facilities, like failure to supply the summary, is punishable by a fine of up to £2500.

Very similar rules apply where the lease allows, or requires, the freeholder to take out insurance against certain contingencies, such as major repair, and to recover the premiums through the service charge.

149

This is not unreasonable and will, indeed, often be in the interests of leaseholders. The danger is, however, that the freeholder, knowing that the premiums are, in effect, being paid by someone else, has no incentive to shop around for the best deal. Section 30A of the Landlord and Tenant Act 1985 therefore lays down that leaseholders, or the secretary of the recognised tenants' association if there is one, may ask the freeholder for information about the policy. Failure to supply it, or to make facilities to inspect relevant documents available if requested to do so, is an offence incurring a fine of up to £2500.

Challenging the reasonableness of a service charge

Any leaseholder liable to pay a service charge, and for that matter any freeholder levying one, may refer the charge to a First Tier Tribunal to determine its reasonableness. This may be done at any time, even when the service in question is merely a proposal by the freeholder (for instance, for future major works). But the FTT will not consider a service charge if:

-    it has already been approved by a court; or
-    if the leaseholder has agreed to refer it to arbitration; or
-    if the leaseholder has agreed it.

The first of these exceptions is obvious and the second is unlikely to apply very often. The third one is the problem: leaseholders should be careful, in their dealings with freeholders, to say or do nothing that could be taken to imply that they agree with any service charge that is in any way doubtful.

The FTT will consider:

o whether the freeholder's costs of services, repairs,

maintenance, insurance, or management are reasonably incurred.

o   whether the services or works are of a reasonable standard; and

o   whether any payment required in advance is reasonable.

The fees for application to a FTT can be obtained from the FTT and will usually change annually. Appeal against a FTT decision is not to the courts but to the Lands Tribunal.

By section 19 of the Landlord and Tenant Act 1985, any service charge deemed unreasonable by the FTT is irrecoverable by the freeholder.

****

Chapter 14

BUYING A FREEHOLD AND EXTENDING A LEASE

In general terms, legislation confers two distinct rights: to purchase the freehold, either individually in relation to leasehold houses, or collectively for a block of flats, or to seek a lease extension. Although these rights are curtailed by the statutory tests for qualification, changes to the legislation, introduced by the Commonhold and Leasehold Reform Act 2002, have made it easier than ever for leaseholders to make a claim.

The requirement that leaseholders must have occupied the property in question for a period of two years (the so-called residence requirement) has largely been swept away and replaced by a new, two-year ownership test. Indeed, in the case of a collective enfranchisement, even the ownership requirement has been removed. Likewise, qualification tests based on the property's ratable values and rent have gone, with the result that higher value houses, for example, may now enfranchise.

The Collective Right to enfranchise
What is it?
This gives the right for tenants of flats acting together to purchase the freehold and any headleases of their building. For the building to qualify under the Act, it must:
• be an independent building or be a part of a building which is capable of independent development; and
152

• contain two or more flats held by qualifying tenants; and
• have at least two thirds of the flats held by qualifying tenants.
In order to be a qualifying tenant, you must have a long lease which means a lease which, when originally granted, was for a term of more than 21 years. However, you must not own three or more flats in the building. You cannot be a qualifying tenant if you hold a business lease.

Notwithstanding the above, the building will not qualify if:
• it comprises four or less units and has a "resident freeholder".
• more than 25% of the internal floor space (excluding common parts) is used for non-residential purposes.
• the building is part of an operational railway.

How do leaseholders prepare for a claim?
Any qualifying tenant can give a notice to his landlord or the managing agent requiring details of the various legal interests in the block. This notice places no commitment on the tenant but the response to the notice should provide the tenant with the information necessary for him to ascertain whether the building contains enough qualifying tenants for it to qualify.

Having established that the building qualifies, it is then advisable to ascertain whether leaseholders have enough tenants who want to participate, both for the purpose of qualifying for enfranchisement and for the purpose of being able to finance the acquisition. To qualify for enfranchisement, leaseholders need to establish that the number of participating tenants comprises not less than one half of all the flats in the building. However, if there are only two flats in the building then both must participate.

When leaseholders have established that the building qualifies and that there is enough qualifying tenants who wish to participate, then there are five further practical steps which should be taken before embarking on the enfranchisement procedure.

First, leaseholders need to establish what it is going to cost by obtaining a valuation. In simple terms, the price to be paid by the participating tenants to purchase the freehold of the building is the aggregate of:

- The building's investment value to the freeholder-the capitalised value of his ground rents and the value of his reversion (being the present freehold vacant possession value deferred for the unexpired term of the lease).
- One half of the marriage value-the increased value attributable to the freehold by virtue of the participating tenants being able to grant themselves extended leases at nil premium and a peppercorn rent. The marriage value attributable to a lease held by a participating tenant will be deemed to be nil if that lease has an unexpired term of more than 80 years at the date that the initial notice is given.
- Compensation for loss of value of other property owned by the freeholder, including development value consequent to the severance of the building from that other property.

The valuation date is the date that the claim notice is given. Value added to the flat of a participating tenant by tenant's improvements is disregarded in the valuation.

For the purposes of calculating price, the tenants should take the advice of a properly qualified surveyor or valuer with experience in the field of enfranchisement and knowledge of the market. In addition to the price and the participating tenants' own legal costs and valuation fees, the claimants will be required to reimburse the freeholder his legal costs and valuation fees.

Secondly, the participators will need to establish how to finance the cost of acquisition. It may, for example, be necessary for several participating tenants to seek a further advance from a Building Society or Bank. In particular, the participators will want to decide who is to finance the purchase of the non-participators' flats and on what basis.

Thirdly, it will be necessary to establish what vehicle the participating tenants should use to buy the freehold and how they will establish and regulate the relationship between themselves. In most cases, this is likely to be through a company structure, although in some circumstances a trust might be more appropriate. It should be noted that the participating tenants do not all have to have equal shares, so that the proportion of the shareholdings will be a matter for negotiation between them.

Fourthly, the participating tenants should seek advice to establish whether there are tax implications to the transaction, both in relation to their individual positions and in relation to the vehicle chosen to buy the freehold.

Finally, the collective enfranchisement legislation provides no guidance or controls on the way in which the participating tenants should work together to acquire the freehold. Since the purchase may well involve substantial sums of money and is likely to take time to complete and, during this time, the participating tenants will be heavily reliant on each other for the performance of tasks within strict limits, it is strongly advised that, before embarking on a claim, the participating tenants should enter into a formal agreement (called a participation agreement) in order to regulate the relationship between them during the course of the claim.

How is the claim made?

It is important to be aware that most of the time limits imposed on the procedural stages of the claim are strict and a failure to do something within the required time frame can have dire consequences for the defaulter. It is therefore essential that, by the time leaseholders reach the next stage of the procedure, they are well organised and backed by expert professional advice.

The reason for this is that the next procedural step is the service by the participating tenants on the landlord of what the Act calls the initial notice – the notice which claims the right to collective enfranchisement. Costs start to run against the tenants from the time they serve the initial notice. Amongst other things this notice must specify:

• the extent of the property to be acquired – supported by a plan.
• full particulars of all the qualifying tenants in the building –
not just the participating tenants.
• the price being offered for the freehold – the offer should be genuine.
• the name and address of the nominee purchaser – the person or company nominated by the participating tenants to conduct the negotiations and to buy the freehold on their behalf.
• the date by which the freeholder must give his counter-notice, being a date not less than two months from the date of the service of the initial notice.

The freeholder is likely to respond with a procedural notice requiring the participating tenants to deduce title. The freeholder's valuer is also likely to inspect the building for the purpose of carrying out a valuation.

Within the period specified in the initial notice, the freeholder must serve his counter-notice. First and foremost, this must state whether the claim is admitted. If it is not, then the participating tenants must decide if they wish to dispute the rejection through the courts.

There are circumstances where the freeholder can resist a claim on the ground of redevelopment.

If the claim is admitted, then the counter-notice must state, amongst other things:

• which of the proposals contained in the initial notice are acceptable.
• which of the proposals contained in the initial notice are not acceptable and what are the freeholder's counter-proposals – particularly on price.
• whether the freeholder wants a leaseback on any units in the building not held by a qualifying tenant (for example, a flat subject to a short-term tenancy or a commercial unit).
• compensation for loss in value of other property owned by the freeholder, including development value consequent to sale

Disputes

If any terms of acquisition (including the price) remain in dispute after two months following the date of the counter-notice, then either party can apply to the leasehold valuation tribunal for the matter in dispute to be determined.

This application must be made within six months following the date of the counter-notice or the claim is lost. Most claims are settled by negotiation. If a First Tier Tribunal is required to decide, then there is a right to appeal that decision to the Lands Tribunal if permission is given to do so.

Completion

Once the terms of acquisition have been agreed or determined by the FTT tribunal, then the matter reverts to a conveyancing transaction with the parties entering a sale contract on the terms agreed or determined and thence to completion.

If the matter proceeds to completion, then the participating tenants, through their nominee purchaser, will become the freeholder of the building, subject to the various flat leases. In effect, the participating tenants will replace the existing freeholder. This will put them in a position to grant themselves extended leases.

There may be taxation consequences on granting an extended lease, particularly for second homeowners. There will also be responsibilities. The participating tenants will become responsible for the management of the building and the administration of the service charge account in accordance with the covenants in the original leases.

If the nominee purchaser is a company, all participators will be shareholders, and some will be officers of that company. These are all matters on which clear professional advice will be needed. It is important to note that an individual tenant has no right to become a participating tenant – even if he is a qualifying tenant. It is a matter for the tenants to resolve between themselves. Leaseholders can always ask to be allowed to join in, but they will have no remedy if refused.

The individual right to extend leases
What is it?

The individual right to a statutory lease extension applies to all qualifying tenants of flats. The condition is that a person must be the tenant of a flat which they hold on a long lease (i.e., a lease for an original term more than 21 years). Furthermore, they must have owned the lease for at least two years before the date of the claim. To

158

claim the lease extension, there is no limit to the number of flats a leaseholder may own in the building, and they may extend any or all of them provided that the conditions are met. However, a person cannot be a qualifying tenant if they hold a business lease.

Prior to the 2002 Act, the personal representatives of a deceased tenant had no rights to make a claim, even where the deceased tenant was able to fulfil the qualifying conditions. However, such personal representatives can now make a claim provided that the right is exercised within a period of two years from the date of grant of probate.

If a leaseholder qualifies, then they will be entitled to acquire a new extended lease in substitution for their existing lease. This extended lease will be for a term expiring 90 years after the end of the current lease and will reserve a peppercorn rent throughout the term.

Broadly, the lease will otherwise be on the same terms as the existing lease, but the landlord will have certain additional redevelopment rights, exercisable within 12 months before the expiration of the current lease term and within 5 years before the expiration of the extended lease.

The price

The price to be paid for the new lease will be the aggregate of:

• the diminution in value of the landlord's interest in the flat, consequent on the grant of the extended lease; being the capitalised value of the landlord's ground rent and the value of his reversion (being the present near-freehold vacant possession value deferred for the unexpired lease term);

• 50% of the marriage value (the additional value released by the tenant's ability to merge the extended lease with the existing lease) must be paid to the landlord although the marriage value will be

159

deemed to be nil if the existing lease has an unexpired term of more than 80 years at the date of the claim.
• compensation for loss in value of other property owned by the freeholder, including development value, consequent on the grant of the new lease

The valuation date is the date of the claim notice. In addition to the price and the tenant's own legal costs and valuation fees, leaseholders will also be required to reimburse the freeholder their legal costs and valuation fees.

Making the claim
The procedure to be followed is very similar to that for collective enfranchisement. It is therefore important to be aware that most of the time limits imposed on the procedural stages of the claim are strict and a failure to do something within the required time frame can have dire consequences for the defaulter.

The qualifying tenant can serve a preliminary notice to obtain information. Thereafter, he serves his notice of claim (in this case called the tenant's notice of claim) which amongst other things needs to state:

• a description of the flat – but not necessarily with a plan.
• sufficient particulars to establish that the lease qualifies.
• the premium being offered – it must be a bona fide offer.
• the terms of the new lease.
• the date by which the landlord must give the counter-notice, being a date not less than two months from the date of service of the tenant's notice.

The landlord is likely to respond with a procedural notice requiring payment of a deposit (equal to 10% of the premium being offered) and asking the tenant to deduce title. The landlord's valuer is also likely to inspect the flat for the purpose of carrying out a valuation.

Within the period specified in the tenant's notice, the landlord must serve his counter-notice. First and foremost, this must state whether the claim is admitted. If it is not, then the tenant must decide if he wishes to dispute the rejection through the courts. However, unlike a collective enfranchisement claim where the nominee purchaser makes the application to the court in these circumstances, in the case of the statutory lease extension, it is the landlord who makes the application if he has refused the claim.

Disputes

If either the terms of the lease or the premium remains in dispute after two months following the date of the counter-notice, then either party can apply to the leasehold valuation tribunal for the matter in dispute to be determined.

This application must be made within six months following the date of the counter-notice or the claim is lost. Most claims are settled by negotiation. If a First Tier Tribunal is required to decide, then there is a right to appeal that decision to the Lands Tribunal if permission is given to do so

Completion

Once the terms of the lease and the premium have been agreed or determined by the FTT then the matter reverts to a conveyancing transaction with the parties proceeding to completion of the new lease. The tenant can withdraw at any time and there are provisions for the tenant's notice to be considered withdrawn if certain strict time

161

limits are not met by the tenant. As in collective enfranchisement, the tenant is on risk as to costs as from the date of his tenant's notice, so it is essential to be prepared and to be properly advised before starting down the road to an extension. A tenant's notice is capable of being assigned but only in conjunction with a contemporaneous assignment of the lease. It is common for a seller to serve a notice and then sell that notice with the lease to a purchaser, who will take over the claim. There is no limit to the number of times that a tenant can exercise this right – so long as he is prepared to pay the costs for doing so.

Enfranchisement of Houses-Leasehold Reform Act 1967

The Leasehold Reform Act 1967 gives the tenant of a leasehold house who fulfils certain rules of qualification the right to acquire the freehold and any intermediate leases.

The extended lease option

Following the 2002 Act, all tenancies extended under the 1967 Act now have security of tenure. Furthermore, the tenant under an extended lease now has the right to acquire the freehold, if he otherwise fulfils the qualifying conditions; in such cases, the purchase price will be determined in accordance with section 9(1C) but with modified assumptions.

****

Chapter 15

THE LAW AND MOBILE (PARK) HOMES

Introduction to park homes

Park Home is the commonly used term for a mobile home (caravan) on a protected site within the meaning of the Mobile Homes Act 1983 (the 1983 Act). A protected site is one that is required to be licensed by a local authority under Part 1 of the Caravan Sites and Control of Development Act 1960 which covers most sites containing wholly residential park homes or a mixture of residential and holiday homes.

If someone has an agreement to live in a 'park home' as their only or main residence on a protected site, then they will have the benefit of the rights and protections provided by the 1983 Act which implies several important terms into their agreement. These cover such matters as to how the agreement can be terminated, how the annual 'pitch fee' can be changed and the process that needs to be followed when buying or selling (or gifting) the home.

Changes to implied rights under the 1983 Act came into effect on 26 May 2013. These concern the buying, selling, or gifting of a park home and the pitch fee review process. Further changes to the licensing of park homes came into effect on 1 April 2014, giving local authorities greater powers to enforce compliance with site licence conditions.

The right to a written agreement and a statement of rights

The site owner must give a person a statement of their legal rights and the terms of their agreement. The agreement cannot change their rights under the Mobile Homes Act. the owner or the site owner can apply to change the terms of the agreement within six months of the issue of the original agreement. Either side can apply to the county court or an arbitrator, if they cannot agree the terms.

Buying a park home from the site owner

The changes made by the Mobile Homes Act 2013 will have little impact upon the process of purchasing a park home from the site owner. Where buying a park home directly from the site owner (or bringing one's own home onto the site) owners can seek to negotiate the terms of their agreement with the site owner, although certain terms will be implied into the agreement by the 1983 Act.

What a person should receive

The site owner should provide the owner with a written statement setting out the specific terms of their agreement to live in their park home on the site. This must be given to them 28 days before they sign the agreement (or if there is no such agreement at least 28 days before occupation).

The terms of the written statement will apply whether they are part of any written agreement with the site owner.

The form of the written statement has been prescribed by regulations. The latest version is contained in the Mobile Homes (Written Statement) (England) Regulations 2011 which applies to written statements provided after 30 April 2011.

The written statement contains information about rights and the particulars of the agreement such as the details of the pitch on which the park home rests, the pitch fee, The terms that are implied into the agreement under the 1983 Act including repairing responsibilities and any additional express terms that it is proposed should be included in

164

the agreement. If a person does not receive a written statement, then any express terms in the agreement such as those providing for the payment of the pitch fee cannot be enforced by the site owner. A person can apply to a tribunal for an order that the written statement is provided by the site owner. The form that should be used is Form PH1.

Other rules
There will often be specific rules that will apply to a particular site (site rules) which deal with such matters as any age restrictions, the use of car parking areas and keeping pets.

Changing the terms of the agreement
An owner or the site owner can apply to a tribunal to delete, vary or add an express term within the first six months of the original agreement being made. The form that should be used is Form PH2.

Buying a park home from an existing homeowner
Significant changes have been made by the Mobile Homes Act 2013 to the process by which a mobile home is bought and sold in England following changes made by the Mobile Homes Act 2013. These changes mean that as from 26 May 2013 a buyer does not have to have any contact with the site owner before buying the home.

It should be noted that until changes are made to the law that applies in Wales, the consent of the site owner will still be required for a person to purchase a park home there.

What will be the terms of the agreement with the site owner?
A person will be taking over an existing agreement with the site owner and so this will depend upon the agreement that was previously made

with the site owner for the home to be stationed on the site. However certain terms will be implied into the agreement.

The new process for buying a park home in England

New terms concerning the sale of the park home are now being implied into agreements between park homeowners and site owners. These new implied terms vary depending on whether the home was acquired by the current owner on or before 26 May 2013.

However, the changes that have been introduced will mean that in all cases the site owner will have no direct involvement in the sale or gift of a park home and any inconsistent provision in the agreement or site rules will not be enforceable.

The process

Once a person has agreed with the seller to purchase the park home, the seller will be required to serve them with a prescribed notice called a Buyer's Information Form at least 28 days before the sale date. This notice will include prescribed information including the proposed sale price and details about the pitch fee and the site owner.

The other documentation that the seller must also give a person is set out in the above Buyer's Information Form and includes the agreement, site rules, evidence of charges payable for utilities and any survey of the park home.

If the current home owner acquired their park home before 26 May 2013, the purchaser and the seller will be required to send to the site owner a Notice of Proposed Sale Form containing their name and, if the site has rules, confirmation that they will comply with any site rules concerning age restrictions, the keeping of pets and the parking of vehicles.

The sale can go ahead if the seller does not receive a notification within 21 days of the service of the Notice of Proposed Sale Form that the site owner has applied to a tribunal for a Refusal Order on the grounds that they will not comply with these rules, or there is insufficient evidence of compliance. The seller will have to transfer the pitch agreement (this is called the Assignment) to the purchaser. Both will need to complete an Assignment Form which provides confirmation of the agreed purchase price, the commission payable to the site owner and the pitch fee payable by the new occupier.

The purchaser will be required to provide the site owner with details of the seller's forwarding address when they notify the site owner that they are the new owner of the home. They must therefore ensure that the seller provides them with a forwarding address.

The seller will need to retain 10% of the purchase price to pay to the site owner, although this does not become payable until the site owner has provided his bank details following the service of the Notice of Assignment (see below).

There will be no need to inform the site owner of the sale where the home was acquired by the seller after 26 May 2013. Within seven days of the assignment, the purchaser must complete and send a Notice of Assignment form to the site owner with documentary evidence of the price paid for the park home.

As soon as is practicable after receipt of the Notice of Assignment, the site owner must provide the purchaser with details of their bank account into which the commission should be paid. The payment of the commission does not become due until the site owner has provided his bank details. On receipt of the details, the purchaser will have seven days to pay the commission into the site owner's bank account.

Gifting a park home to family member

The Mobile Homes Act 1983 enables a park homeowner to assign their agreement with the site owner to a member of their family (this is defined in the Mobile Homes Act 1983 and includes spouse, parent, child, grandparent, grandchild and brother or sister). The changes introduced by the Mobile Homes Act 2013 to the process whereby a park home in England can be gifted to a family member mirror those for the sale of a park home. This means that the site owner is not required to approve the gift and any inconsistent provision in the agreement or site rules will not be enforceable.

Please note that until changes are made to the law in Wales, the consent of the site owner will be required for a gift of a park home to a family member there.

The process for receiving a gift of a park home in England

A person should receive a copy of the agreement, site rules, evidence of the charges payable for utilities and any survey of the park home as for a normal sale (although there is no requirement for the current occupier to provide the giftee with the Buyer's Information Form).

Informing the site owner about the gift of the home

Where the current occupier (the family member gifting the home to you) acquired the park home before 26 May 2013, they will need to complete and send a Notice of Proposed Gift to the site owner providing details of how they are related to him or her, together with supporting documentary evidence such as a birth or marriage certificate.

Where there are site rules concerning the age of the occupant, the keeping of pets and the parking of vehicles, the person making the gift will need to provide information to the site owner confirming that they are able to comply with these rules.

The family member gifting the park home can then proceed with the assignment provided that he has not been informed by the site owner within 21 days of the service of the Notice of Proposed Gift that an application has been made to a First-tier Tribunal (Property Chamber) for a Refusal Order, or if he has already been informed that there is no objection to the proposed gift.

Is there anything else that needs to be done?
The final stage is for the giftee to complete a Notice of Assignment which they as the new owner must send to the site owner within seven days of the assignment.

No commission will be payable on the gift of a park home to a family member

Protection from eviction
The Mobile Homes Act 1983, as amended by the Housing Act 2004, gives owners the right to keep their homes on the site they occupy indefinitely. There can only be a fixed time limit on the agreement if the site owner's planning permission, or right to use the land, is itself limited to a fixed period. If the time limit is later extended, then so is the owners right to stay there. The resident can bring the agreement to an end by giving at least four weeks notice in writing. The site owner can only bring the agreement to an end by applying to the county court or to an arbitrator. There are only three grounds on which the site owner can seek to end an agreement:

- the person is not living in the mobile home as their main residence.

- The mobile home is having a detrimental effect on the site because of its age or condition or is likely to have this effect within the next five years. The site owner can only try to use this ground for ending the agreement once in any five-year period, starting from the date the agreement began.
- The person has broken one of the terms of the agreement and the court or the arbitrator thinks it is reasonable to end the agreement. The site owner must first tell them that they have broken the agreement and give them reasonable time to put things right.

If the site owner can prove to the court or the arbitrator that the agreement should be ended for one of these reasons, the site owner can then get an eviction order from the courts. Arbitrators cannot make eviction orders. The site owner can normally go to court to end the agreement and for an eviction order at the same time.

If the site is privately owned, the court can suspend an eviction order for up to one year but cannot suspend it if the site is owned by the local council. It is a criminal offence for the site owner to evict a person without a court order, to harass or threaten them or to cut off services such as gas, electricity, or water to get them to leave.

The site owner can only make a person move to another part of the site if:

their agreement says that this can be done

- The new pitch is broadly comparable to the old one
- The site owner pays all the costs.

Other rights and obligations-Charges-Pitch fee

A person must pay a 'pitch fee' to the park owner to rent the land their park home sits on. The park owner can propose to change it once a year. They must give 28 days' notice in writing. The person or the park owner can apply to a tribunal to decide the pitch fee if they can't agree on it.

Gas, water, electricity, and liquefied petroleum gas (LPG)

The Office of the Gas and Electricity Markets (Ofgem) sets the amount the park owner can charge for gas and electricity. The park owner can't charge more for gas and electricity than they paid for it, including any connection charges. For water, the park owner can only charge what the water company charges and a reasonable administration fee. Charges for LPG aren't regulated.

Park improvements

If the park owner plans to make improvements, they must:

- give at least 28 days' notice in writing and let the person know how they can comment on the plans
- tell them if it will affect the pitch fee

They can go ahead with improvements even if most residents disagree. The park owner can sometimes recover improvement costs through a pitch fee increase. If a person disagrees, they can apply to a tribunal.

Residents' associations

park homeowners can set up a 'qualifying' residents' association to represent homeowners in the mobile home park where they live. Qualifying residents' associations have certain rights and park owners should consult the residents' association when they want to spend money on improvements or change how they run the park.

Park owners must give at least 28 days' notice of any changes and take the association's concerns into account before they make changes.

Setting up a qualifying residents' association

The association must include at least half of the homeowners in the park. Residents who rent their homes can't join. Residents must keep certain records and documents, like:

- an up-to-date list of members
- a constitution
- any other rules of the association

Residents must elect a:
- chairman
- secretary
- treasurer

The chairman, secretary and treasurer can make administrative decisions. Members should vote on all other decisions. residents need to ask the park owner to 'acknowledge' the association. they can apply to a tribunal if they refuse. They can order the park owner to acknowledge the association. the association can continue to meet if it doesn't meet the qualifying conditions, but the park owner won't have to talk to the association about park operations and management.

7. Settling disputes

If residents have a dispute with the park owner that they can't work out, they can apply to a tribunal. Decisions made by the tribunal are legally binding.

172

The tribunal can settle certain disputes, eg:
- changing a residence agreement
- changing the pitch fee
- moving a park home
- damage and repairs to the site
- transferring ownership of a park home to someone else

****

Chapter 16

Residential Moorings

Living on a boat

Living on a boat can be cheaper than renting a flat or house, but there aren't many vacant permanent moorings.

Boat licences and fees

You usually need a boat licence. This costs around £500 to £1,000 per year and gives you permission to use the waterways. You must display the licence on both sides of your boat. You also need to pay a mooring fee if you rent a mooring.

Moorings for boats

Very few permanent residential moorings for boats are available. You can sometimes buy a boat with an all-year-round residential mooring. You can rent a residential mooring in a private marina or from the navigation authority. Some mooring operators won't rent out a mooring to a boat owner who lives permanently on their boat. Some boat dwellers live on permanent moorings that are not for residential use. If you use a non-residential mooring as your home, the local authority can take legal action to move you on.

Continuous cruising

Many dwellers do not have a permanent mooring. This is sometimes called continuous cruising. A continuous cruiser can usually moor in one spot for up to 14 days. You may only be able to moor for 48 hours in some areas. This can be difficult if you need to live in the same area because of work or school. Boats are allowed to moor at most places on canal towpaths. There are more restrictions on rivers. Moorings for winter (from November to March) are available in some locations.

Renting a houseboat

If you rent a boat, make sure it is rented to you with a residential mooring. Most all-year-round residential moorings do not allow boats to be rented out. Check that the site owner has given your landlord permission for you to stay there.

Paying council tax for a houseboat

You may have to pay council tax if you live on a houseboat with a residential mooring.

Housing benefit

If you live on a houseboat, you can **claim housing benefit** or **universal credit** to help pay your mooring fees or rent, if you rent rather than own it. You can't claim housing benefit for a continuous cruiser licence.

Useful information on houseboats

Get legal advice if you're told you can no longer stay where you're moored. Use the **Law Society Directory** to find legal help in your area. You can also contact the:

* **National Bargee Travellers Association**
* **Canal & River Trust**

****

Chapter 17

AGRICULTURAL TENANCIES

If a person rents agricultural land or buildings to run a farm business, they may have an agricultural tenancy agreement. Every agricultural tenancy agreement is unique. We refer here to 2 types of agricultural tenancies governed by legislation:

- Farm Business Tenancies governed by the Agricultural Tenancies Act 1995 - those agreed after 1 September 1995
- 1986 Act Tenancies governed by the Agricultural Holdings Act 1986 - those agreed before 1 September 1995

Farm Business Tenancies
A tenancy is a Farm Business Tenancy if at least part of the tenanted land is farmed throughout the life of the tenancy. The tenancy must also meet one of these 2 conditions:

- if the tenancy is primarily agricultural to start with, the landlord and tenant can exchange notices before the tenancy begins confirming they intend it to remain a Farm Business Tenancy throughout - this lets tenants diversify away from agriculture where the terms of the tenancy agreement allow this
- if the landlord and tenant don't exchange notices before the tenancy begins, the tenancy business must be primarily agricultural to be considered a Farm Business Tenancy

Farm Business Tenancy rent reviews

Landlords and tenants can negotiate their own rent levels and decide whether they want to have rent reviews. Either the landlord or tenant can demand a rent review every 3 years by law.

However, landlords and tenants can agree on how often a rent review should take place – this agreement replaces the law. For example, tenants can agree on a rent review every 4 years.

Farm Business Tenancy compensation

As a farm business tenant, a person is entitled to compensation at the end of a tenancy for:

- physical improvements they made to a holding (provided the landlord has given consent to the improvements)
- changes that increase the value of the holding (provided they are left behind when the tenant leaves)

Owners can agree in writing an upper limit on the amount of compensation, usually equal to the tenant's cost in making the improvements.

Ending a Farm Business Tenancy

Landlords and tenants of a Farm Business Tenancy can end the tenancy by issuing a notice to quit. The minimum notice period to quit is 12 months

1986 Act agricultural tenancies

Agricultural tenancies agreed before 1 September 1995 are known as 1986 Act Tenancies. They're also sometimes referred to as Full

Agricultural Tenancies (FATs) or Agricultural Holdings Act tenancies (AHAs).

These tenancies usually have lifetime security of tenure and those granted before 12 July 1984 also carry statutory succession rights, on death or retirement. This means a close relative of a deceased tenant can apply for succession to the tenancy within 3 months of the tenant's death.

Applying for succession stops any notice to quit given by the landlord on the tenant's death. Two tenancies by succession can be granted, so it's possible for the tenant's family to work the holding for 3 generations. Farmers with a tenancy granted before 12 July 1984 can also name an eligible successor such as a close relative who can apply to take over the holding when they retire.

1986 Act Tenancies rent reviews

The landlord or tenant has the right to a rent review 3 years after either the:

- start of a tenancy
- previous rent review

If land is added to or removed from a holding, then the next rent review must be either at least 3 years from one of the following:

- the date the original tenancy began
- from the date of the previous rent review for the original tenancy

This rent review must happen even if the rent has changed to reflect changes to the amount of land on the holding.

1986 Act Tenancies compensation
Under the 1986 Act Tenancy agreements the tenant is entitled to compensation at the end of their tenancy for the following:
- major long-term improvements
- short-term improvements
- 'tenant right'

Major long-term improvements
These include:
- making or planting water meadows
- planting orchards
- erecting or altering buildings
- constructing silos, roads, or bridges
- repairs to fixed equipment

Short-term improvements
These include:
- mole drainage
- protecting fruit trees against animals
- clay burning
- liming and chalking of land
- applying manure, fertiliser, soil improvers and digestate to the land (in England)

'Tenant right'
These include:
- the value of growing crops
- the costs of husbandry, such as sowing seeds and cultivations
- compensation for disturbance where a landlord terminates the tenancy with a notice to quit

The amount of compensation is measured by the increase in value to the holding made by the improvements. The landlord may also claim compensation for disrepair - usually the cost of repairing any damage.

Dispute procedures

Where a landlord or a tenant has a dispute relating to an Agricultural Tenancy (either a 1986 Act Tenancy or a Farm Business Tenancy) they can use third-party expert determination or arbitration procedures.

Arbitration is the private legal settlement of a dispute by an independent, professional arbitrator who can involve either of the following:

- a tribunal hearing where both sides present evidence and testimony
- the 2 parties agreeing to resolve the dispute using written arbitration procedures, avoiding the time and costs of a hearing

If a landlord and tenant can't agree on the appointment of an arbitrator, either of them can apply to the President of the Royal Institution of Chartered Surveyors (RICS) to make an appointment on their behalf for an arbitrator to:

- decide a rent review dispute
- resolve a dispute other than a rent review

Contacts

Farmers can get further information on agricultural tenancy issues from the Tenant Farmers Association and the National Farmers Union. Please note that the law differs in Scotland and Wales, information on which can be obtained from these sites.

Ch. 18

Housing Advice Generally

Although this book has comprehensively detailed all areas of housing, it could be that you feel you need more specific Housing Advice.

General advice
Citizens Advice Bureaus, which are situated throughout the U.K., provide advice on all problems, including housing and other matters such as legal, welfare benefits and relationship breakdown. If appropriate they can refer you for more specialist help to a solicitor or advice agency. This advice is free of charge. To find a local office, look in the telephone directory under National Association of Citizens Advice Bureau. Shelter UK is also a useful website www.shelter.org.uk.

Housing Advice Centres
In many areas there are specialist advice centres offering housing aid and advice. The service they offer varies from one-off information to detailed help over a long period.

There are two main types of housing advice centres, Local council housing aid centres which can advise on all kinds of problems, although they will not be able to act against their own council. Independent housing aid centres may be better equipped to do this. These centres can offer detailed assistance over a length of time and one-off advice. There are several independent housing aid centres throughout the country operated by Shelter. You should contact Shelter for your nearest centre.

Other specialist advice

Law centres-they offer free advice and can sometimes represent you in court. They can usually advise on all aspects of law and advise battered women. They cannot, however, take divorce cases. For this you will need a solicitor. Shelter can provide a list of law centres.

For advice on welfare rights, you should try the local council, who may employ a welfare rights advisor. Advisers can also contact the advice line which is run by the Child Poverty Action Group.

For women's rights Women's Aid (England), https://www.womensaid.org.uk and Welsh Women's Aid, https://www.welshwomensaid.org.uk, refer battered women, with or without children, to refuges. They can put you in touch with sympathetic solicitors and local women's aid groups and can offer a range of other advice, such as welfare benefits.

For immigration advice, the Joint Council for the Welfare of Immigrants, https://www.jcwi.org.uk offers advice on all types of problems connected with immigration and nationality.

The Refugee Council has an advice service for refugees and asylum seekers.

https://www.refugeecouncil.org.uk

https://www.scottishrefugeecouncil.org.uk

Advice from solicitors

Solicitors can advise you on all aspects of the law, represent you in certain courts and, if necessary, get a barrister to represent you. It is best to find a solicitor who specialises in housing rights as they usually have a wider knowledge of specific areas. You can get a list of solicitors who specialise in housing law from the Community Legal Service (CLS) Directory in your local library. The list is also on the CLS website. Citizens Advice Bureaus can also supply specialist solicitor details.

Free advice and help

The Legal Help Scheme, whilst also being squeezed, can pay for up to two hours worth of free advice and assistance and for matrimonial cases up to three hours. The scheme is means tested and you must come within the limits of the scheme to qualify. For details of the scheme, you should approach a Citizens Advice Bureau or a solicitor's practice operating the scheme. You must have reasonable grounds for defending an action. In certain cases, if you succeed in obtaining cash compensation then you may have to pay a proportion of it back, this is known as the *statutory charge.*

****

Useful Websites

Shelter
https://england.shelter.org.uk/housing_advice

https//scotland.shelter.org.uk
Housing advice Wales
https://gov.wales/housing

Housing Advice Northern Ireland
https://www.housingadviceni.org

Citizens Advice Service
https://www.citizensadvice.org.uk

Leasehold Advisory Service
https://www.lease-advice.org

Care home rights and obligations
https://england.shelter.org.uk/.../care_homes_for_older_people

****

Index

****